Tartans

Frederickton to MacNeil

MW00862100

William H. Johnston and Philip D. Smith, Jr.

4880 Lower Valley Road, Atglen, PA 19310 USA

Acknowledgments

Our thanks to: Eli O'Carroll, Chief of Clan Cian/O'Carroll; Graham Carson of Rusco, Bt.; Kenneth Dalgliesh, D.C. Dalgliesh & Sons; Alistair Buchan, Lochcarron Mills; Blair Macnaughton, The House of Edgar; Trudi Mann, "Caithness" and "Highland I, II"; Nicholas Steward, "Massachusetts"; Stanley Burch, "U.S. Postal Service"; Robin Birch, "Birch"; Rosalind Jones, "Jones"; Debborah Allen "Alan/Allen"; Peter MacDonald; Anthony Murray; Alex Lumsden; "Shep" Shepherd; Janice Crook; Marjorie Warren; Bob Martin; Ralf Hartwell, "New Hampshire"; and the many, many others who made this work possible.

Title Page:

Grant tartan, "ancient colors."

Copyright © 1999 by William H. Johnston and Philip D. Smith, Jr.
Library of Congress Catalog Card Number: 99-65299

All rights reserved. No part of this work may be reproduced or used in any form or by any means—graphic, electronic, or mechanical, including photocopying or information storage and retrieval systems—without written permission from the copyright holder.
"Schiffer," "Schiffer Publishing Ltd. & Design," and the "Design of pen and ink well" are registered trademarks of Schiffer Publishing Ltd.

Designed by Ian C. Robertson
Type set in LydianBT/ZapfHumanist601BT

ISBN: 0-7643-0962-5
Printed in China

Published by Schiffer Publishing Ltd.
4880 Lower Valley Road
Atglen, PA 19310
Phone: (610) 593-1777; Fax: (610) 593-2002
E-mail: Schifferbk@aol.com
Please visit our web site catalog at **www.schifferbooks.com**

In Europe, Schiffer books are distributed by Bushwood Books
6 Marksbury Avenue Kew Gardens
Surrey TW9 4JF England
Phone: 44 (0)181 392-8585; Fax: 44 (0)181 392-9876
E-mail: Bushwd@aol.com

Drawing of a cottage in Islay.

Introduction

The "clan tartan myth," so called because of its tenuous foundation but tenacious appeal, had its roots in the late 1600s. At that time the Highlands of Scotland were less known to English and other Europeans than were the Americas. Visitors to the Americas brought back vivid tales and wrote many books, but few and less frequent visitors traveled to the northern edge of the island called Britain.

One of the earliest writers to describe the Highlanders was Daniel DeFoe, the eighteenth century version of a "war correspondent" in Scotland. His description of the Highland soldiers was that they resembled a bunch of "Merry Andrews"—"clowns" in modern parlance. This was certainly a reference to tartan—and may have illustrated that there was little uniformity among the Highlanders' clothing. Martin Martin, a Gaelic speaking Highlander and a factor on the MacLeod estates, ventured to write of the Highlanders in 1695:

> Every isle differs from each other in their fancy of making Plads as to the stripes in breadth and colours. The humour is as different throughout the mainland of the Highlands, in so far that they who have seen those places are able at first view of the man's Plad, so to guess the place of his residence.

Martin's quotation has been used again and again both to justify and to refute the earliest evidence for "district" tartans, those produced by the local weaver in whatever colors he had available, or for "clan" tartans. Presuming that the inhabitants of isolated islands or glens had access to only one weaver and commonly intermarried, the argument may be irrelevant. When there are less than twenty families in a community, intermarriage cannot be uncommon nor is wearing the same "humour" in "stripes and colours."

In 1703 Captain Hamilton of the Inverness garrison reported that the Laird of Grant, "...has ordered 600 of his men in arms, in good order, with

A past Laird of Macnab.

Tartane Coates all of one colour and fashion." This was alarming since at that time the British government had less than two hundred soldiers scattered among two or three garrisons in all of the Highlands. The Grant records include an order by Alexander Grant of Grant in July, 1704. He specified that all of his tenants from ages sixteen to sixty should be ready to appear at the clan gathering place on forty-eight hours notice. Each man was to be

fully armed and dressed in jackets and trousers of tartan in wide stripes of "red and green."

Militating against the "clan" tartan is Grant's postscript, in which he admonishes his factor to be sure that the two MacDonald tenants in Laggan were to be reminded that this summons applied to them. James H. Grant has pointed out that here was no sett (pattern) specified, simply "red and green, broad springed" but that the time constraint of forty-eight hours suggested that the men were expected to have this clothing on hand.

By the early 1700s tartan had become fashionable in the Lowlands, perhaps due to the Act of Union in which Scotland, who lost her king a century earlier, now merged her parliament with that in London. Also contributing may have been sympathy with the Jacobite cause, support of the exiled Stuarts who many Scots viewed as their legitimate kings. This sentiment culminated in the armed "Rising of '45" led by nineteen-year-old Prince Charles Edward Stuart, "Bonnie Prince Charley."

Following the final defeat on Culloden Moor near Inverness in April, 1746, Charles lived a hunted life, changing clothing often and moving from place to place in the Highlands and Islands until rescued by a French ship. Relics of his clothing were carefully preserved by his adherents. These have contributed greatly to our knowledge of tartan. Some of these have become "clan" tartans.

By 1747 tartan had become firmly identified with the Highlands of Scotland and the wearing of tartan was made illegal by the "Act of Proscription." It is said that when the Earl of Kilmarnock, the Lowland head of the Boyd family, was beheaded in London for his part in "The '45," he pulled a tartan cap from his pocket and placed it on his head as he lowered it to the block, saying, "At least I can die a Scot."

Tartan was officially illegal in Scotland for thirty-five years but enforced only briefly and with many exceptions. The firm of Wilson's of Bannockburn, on the very edge of the Highlands, manufactured and sold tartan in the Highlands well before the repeal of the Act of Proscription. Fortunately for tartan historians, many of their records have survived. The concept that specific tartans were identified with certain clans evolved and gained strength during this period.

Once tartan was legal again, collectors began to travel through the Highlands gathering setts. The Highland Society of London wrote to the clan chiefs asking for examples of their clan's tartan. Few knew. In 1822 King George IV visited Scotland—the first visit of a monarch in a hundred and fifty years. With the direction from Sir Walter Scott that all were to be fully dressed in their clan's tartan, chiefs had to scurry around. Some knew, but others turned to commercial firms. The Drummonds, for example, showed up in the "Grant" tartan and continued that usage for many years.

Many clan tartans in use today depend on thread counts taken from the portrait of a single individual. Others depend on fragments saved over the years with the reverence of holy relics. Some appeared or were associated with the Sobieski Stuarts, who in 1842 published a forged book called the *Vestiarium Scoticum*, purporting to show the true clan setts as they existed in the 1500s.

Regimental designs are well known. Still other tartans are of recent design, requested by a family of the name but open to all with that name who wish to wear it. Some district tartans are historically quite old but again may have been so labeled because of a single individual who wore the title of the region or because of the area in which they were found. Credited with being the two oldest known tartans, the "Lennox District" is so named from a portrait of the Countess of Lennox, circa 1575, and the "Ulster District" from clothing found under debris in Antrim in 1956 but dated to circa 1600. We do not know why Wilson's labeled certain tartans as "Dundee" or "Durham." It may have been because they sold well there or were widely worn in that locale. Modern provincial, town, and state tartans continue to proliferate.

Most tartans have two points in common. First, the weaver/designer does his or her work in exchange for money or goods. Second, the work is probably done to clothe a single individual or his immediate family. Early weaver/designers showed considerable skill in their art. Lately, commemorative and other tartans have become fashionable but short lived.

Tartan continues both as a living art form and for strictly commercial purposes. With a conscious interest in "identification" and with the advent of the computer, designs have proliferated until the Scottish Tartans Authority master data base is approaching five thousand setts. Many of these are variations or alternatives. The Victorian Era saw some clans develop not only "Hunting" tartans but also "Mourning" tartans. The twentieth century saw an oxymoronic "Dress Hunting" tartan and special designs for a clan "Bodyguard" and "Chauffeur." Tartan continues in popularity as we enter the twenty-first century.

Almost all tartans reverse the sett around two "pivots," two color stripes that are at central points on the pattern. Since the sett is then mirrored in all directions, the weaver only requires half of the pattern. Pivots in this book are shown in boldface (e.g. **K/4**) and are **full count**—a weaver will have to divide the pivots by two in setting up the loom. A few setts are asymmetrical. In that case, the full sett is shown ending in a row of boldface dots (**...**) This indicates that instead of reversing, the entire sett is to be repeated starting at the left. Traditionally, thread ends are reduced to the minimum of two. However, in this volume thread counts are from actual samples and may be scaled up or down at the fancy of the weaver. In a few cases the designers/owners do not wish the thread counts published.

Tartan is woven commercially in many shades of color. The actual choice of shades is at the discretion of the artist-weaver. Commercial firms often weave tartan in three or four shades—the deeper "modern" colors that actually pre-dated by a century the so-called "ancient" colors. In this book the majority of tartans are illustrated in the "ancient" colors that became popular in the 1950s since they show the pattern better. "Reproduction" colors owe their popularity to Dixon C. Dalgliesh, who developed them after World War II in imitation of the shades found in a piece of tartan buried on Culloden Moor for two centuries. "Weathered" colors attempt to

A depiction of Gordon Castle.

illustrate tartan exposed to the weather. Other mills have unique color palates.

In the thread counts shown in this book, the names of colors are abbreviated. The actual shade is at the discretion of the weaver. When an unusual color is used, it will be spelled in full at the first occurrence within the sett and then assigned a unique abbreviation or continue to be spelled. Abbreviations used are as follows:

Colors:

A	Azure
B	Blue
C	Crimson
G	Green
K	Black
L	Lavender
M	Maroon
N	Gray (Neutral)
P	Purple
R	Red
T	Brown (Tan)
W	White
Y	Yellow

Prefixes:

D	Dark
M	Medium
L	Light

Some terms require definition:

Sett: The pattern of a tartan.
Arisaid: A white based tartan woven for women's wear.
Dress: A tartan incorporating lighter or brighter colors than the ordinary, often white and sometimes to a different sett. Modern Dress Setts are usually for Highland dancers.

Hunting: A tartan woven in darker or duller shades than the ordinary, sometimes to a different sett.
Vestiarium Scoticum: A book published in 1842 purporting to illustrate the clan tartans as they existed in the sixteenth century. Shown to be a forgery, nonetheless many of the tartans illustrated have come into general use.
Clan Originaux: A book published in France in the 1880s containing a number of lovely but unsubstantiated tartans.
Wilson's: Refers to the setts from William Wilson & Sons pattern books from the late 1700s through the 1840s.
Norwich: Patterns from that English firm which flourished in the mid-nineteenth century.
Black Watch: The 42nd Royal Highland Regiment, whose tartans serve as the basis for many other military and civilian tartans.

Our thanks go to the many people who contribute to the Scottish Tartans Authority data base, but particularly to the late John "Jack" Dalgety and to Anthony Murray and Peter MacDonald, with special thanks to J. Alastair Buchan of Lochcarron Mills and Kenneth Dalgliesh of D. C. Dalgliesh & Sons who permitted us to photograph their collections.

The authors apologize for not being able to include every tartan in these volumes. The tartans chosen are representative of the collection in the database of the International Association of Tartan Studies/TECA. Research continues to uncover more of the past; new tartans continue to be designed.

We sincerely hope that you find this second volume of ***Tartans*** worthwhile.

William H. Johnston
President *Emeritus*

Philip D. Smith, Jr., FSA Scot.
President

The International Association of Tartan Studies/TECA, associated with The Scottish Tartans Authority

Right: The River Tweed in Scotland.

Frederickton, New Brunswick: Y/8 R72 LB8 W8 LB8 W8 LB8 G24 DT32 W48 LB4 **P/12**

Ft. William District: DG/34 A4 LG4 A4 K32 A4 K6 DG60 K4 A4 **K/8**

Fulton: B/12 K20 R8 G8 R12 G48 R24 K4 **R/12**

Gala Water: Orange/10 K32 LB16 P24 W4 LG44 **Y/12**

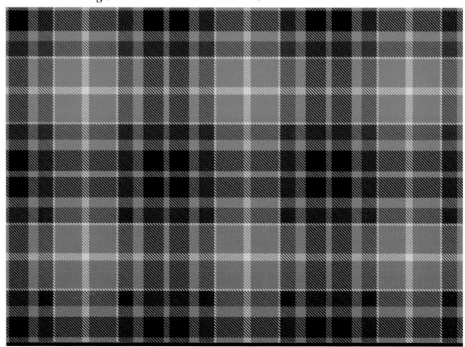

Gala Water District, "Old": K/32 LB16 LP28 G72 **Y/16**

Gala Water, "New"—from Wilson's 1819 pattern book: R/10 K32 A14 P34 W4 G42 **Y/10**

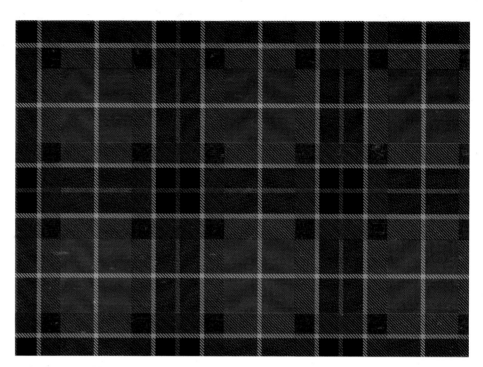

Gala Water, "Old": R/8 K36 LB8 DB36 K60 **Y/8**

Galbraith: K/4 G32 K32 R4 B32 **W/4**

Galicia: A/72 W106 R12 **Gold/16**

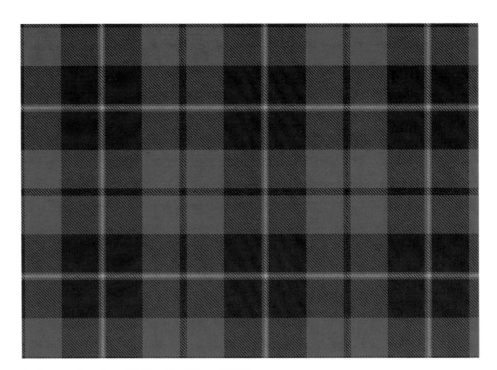

Galloway, Hunting: R/6 K4 G64 DG64 G4 **Y/6**

Galloway, "Red": G/8 R4 B64 R64 B4 **Y/12**

Gammell: B/40 DT4 B4 DT4 B4 DT12 G30 **DT/4**

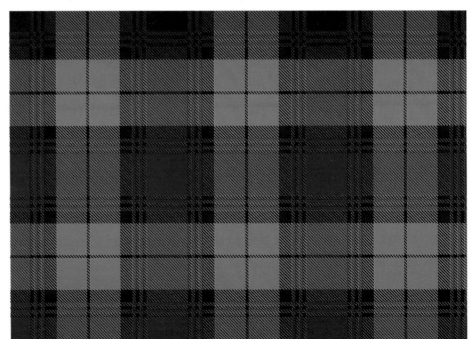

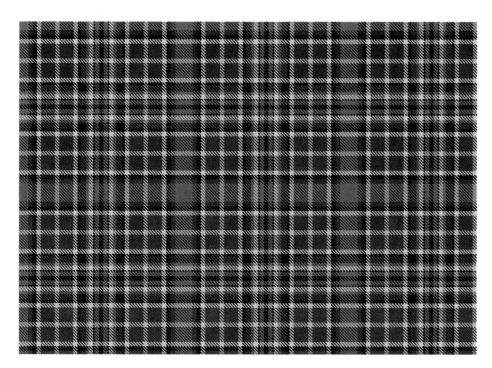

Gayre: LB48 G12 K12 W12 G40 A12 G40 W12 K8 R16 LB8 W12 K4 LB12 **K/12**

Gayre, Dress: B/18 G12 K12 W36 B12 W36 K4 Y4 K4 LR16 G8 W8 G8 LR12 K4 **Y/4**

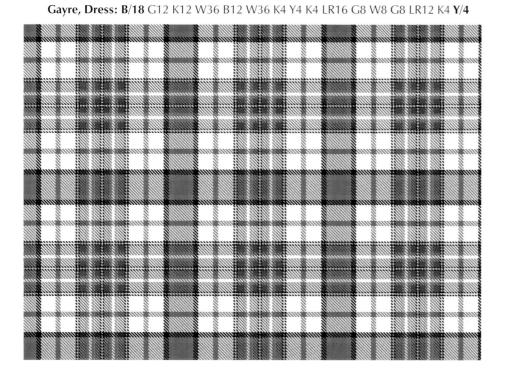

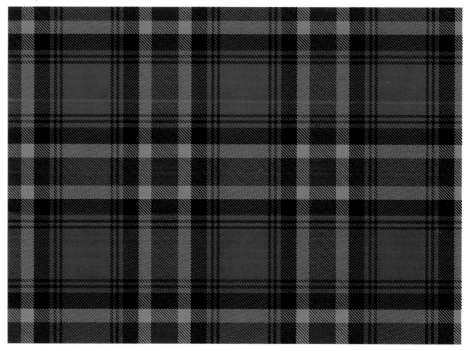

Gayre, Hunting: LB/40 Orange8 K8 N4 LB8 N40 K6 R12 G8 N4 G8 R8 **K/8**

Georgia State: R/68 LB32 K40 DG12 K8 DG8 K8 **DG/160**

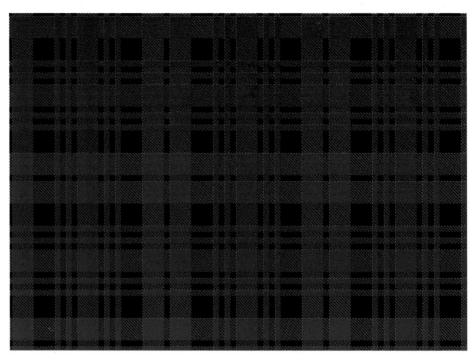

German—a tartan for Germans or those of German descent, D. Ikelman collection: **R/32** K4 R4 K4 R26 K24 R4 K24 R26 K26 R4 **Y/4**

Gibbs / Gibson: LB/8 DG64 W4 LB8 W8 Y16 W8 Y16 W8 LB8 W4 R64 **K/8**

Glasgow Academy: B/28 K8 B8 B8 B8 K28 P28 **K/8**

Glasgow Celtic Society: B/6 T6 B6 T6 B6 T6 B8 G8 K6 G6 K6 G6 K6 G26 R16 G8 B6 **K/12**

Glasgow District: B/4 R8 G54 R44 B50 R8 **G/54**

Glen Orchy District: K/8 G8 R12 B72 R8 G24 R16 W4 B24 R12 G72 R12 K8 **G/8**

Glen Lyon District: B/20 K20 **G/20**

Glen Tilt District: W/4 DG4 DR4 DG56 DR4 LB24 DR44 DG4 DR4 **W/4**

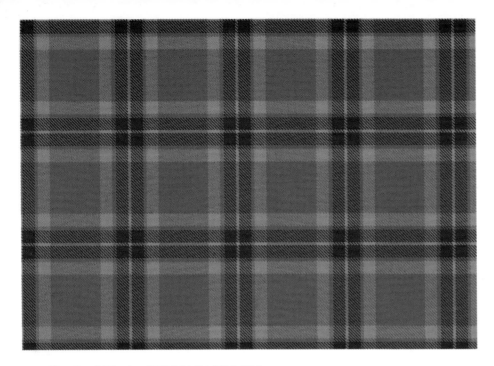

Glen Trool District: LT/6 R20 G6 LT20 **G84**

Gordon: B/32 K4 B4 K4 B4 K20 G32 Y6 G32 K20 B32 K4 **B/4**

Gordon, "Red"—reproduction colors

Gordon of Huntly, Wilson's 1819 sett: K/4 R16 K12 R16 G12 A12 G34 W4 P30 W4 A12 K28 W4 LR14 W4 **P/32**

16

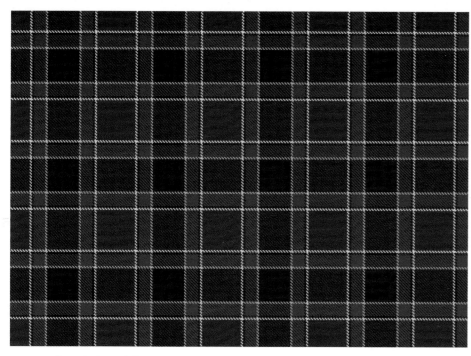

Gordon of Abergeldie, 1723: DR/120 W8 K8 P36 Y8 **K/100**

Gordon of Abergeldie—weathered colors

Gordon of Esselmont: B/56 K4 B4 K4 B6 K24 G40 Y4 G4 Y4 G4 Y4 G40 K24 B36 K4 **B/8**

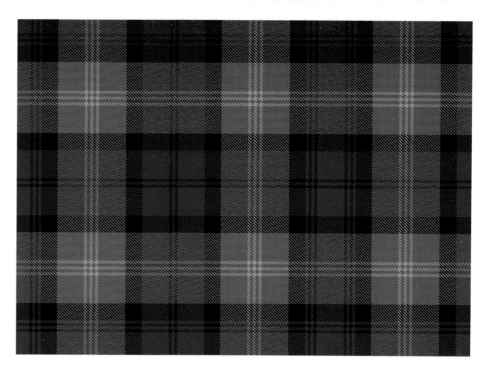

Gow: R/8 G8 R4 B8 **R/8**

17

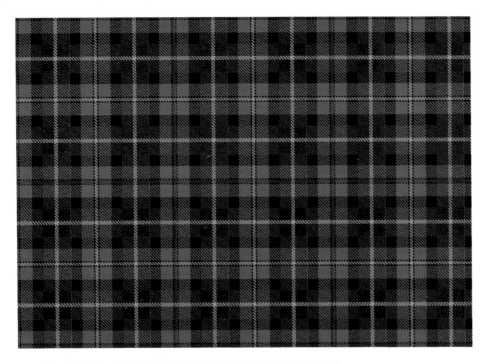

Gow, Hunting: R/8 K4 G28 K24 B28 A8 B28 K24 G28 K4 **Y/8**

Graham of Mentieth: K/4 DB24 K24 DG4 A4 **DG/32**

Graden(e): K/6 G8 W6 G8 W6 G28 K8 **B/16**

Graham of Mentieth—weathered colors

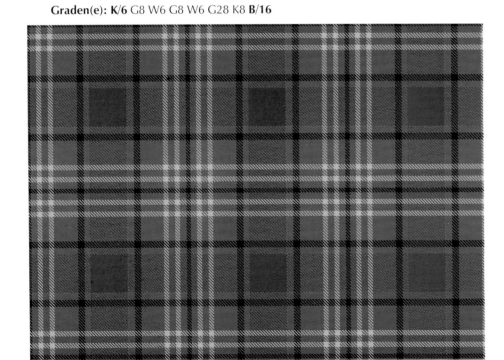

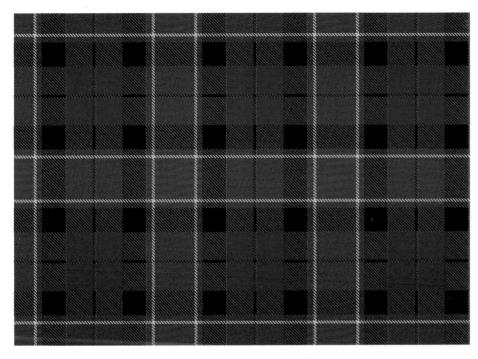

Graham of Mentieth, "Red": R/72 A6 R10 K42 B48 **K/8**

Graham, "Red": A/4 K4 R40 A20 K20 DG40 R40 K4 **A/4**

Graham of Montrose: K/6 B18 K18 G18 W4 G18 **K/18**

Grainger: B/36 K4 B12 K16 G24 **W/4**

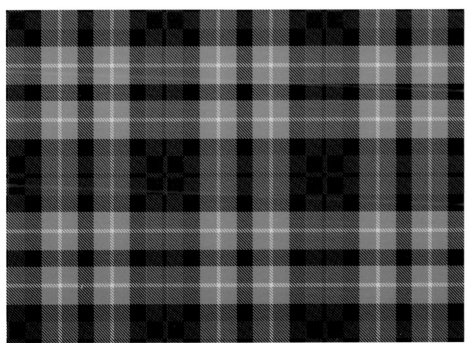

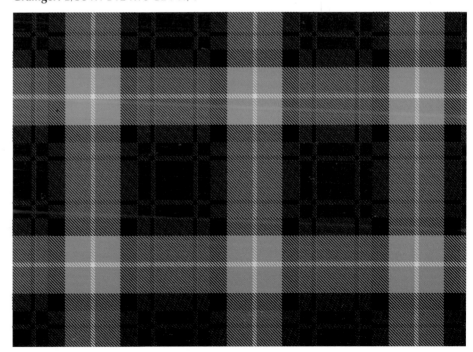

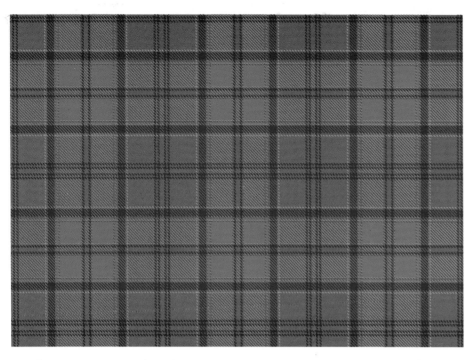

Grant—1860s sett: R/6 K4 R4 K4 R60 A4 R4 DDB16 R4 G4 R4 G48 R4 K4 **R/12**

Grant—reproduction colors

Grant—weathered colors

Grant of Achnarrow, 1780s: **W/8** R8 G6 R24 W28 K4 W4 B8 G12 W56 K6 **W/28**

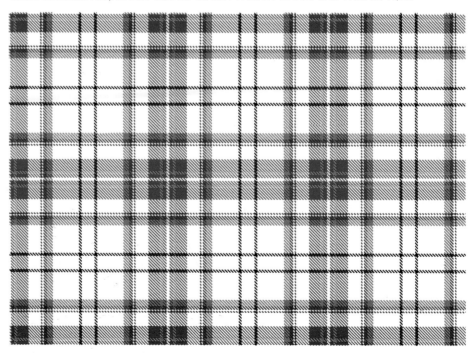

20

Grant of Ballindalloch: R/20 B12 R12 B20 R48 A20 R12 B20 R12 G12 R12 G64 R12 B12 **R/20**

Grant of Monymusk, Cockburn collection: R/24 G6 R24 K18 R10 B32 R8 G32 R6 G32 R6 G32 **R/24**

Grant of Rothiemurchas: R/2 G2 R64 B64 R16 G2 R2 G2 R16 G64 R64 G2 **R/2**

Grant of Rothiemurchas, Hunting: B/44 K8 B8 K8 B8 K44 G44 R10 G12 K4 **Y/6**

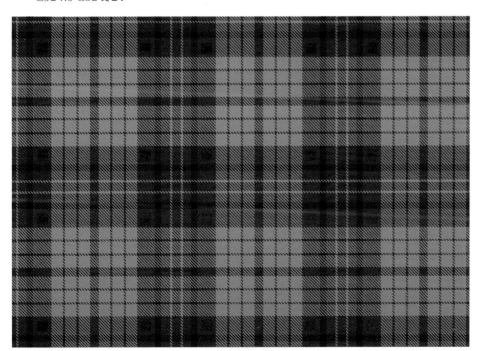

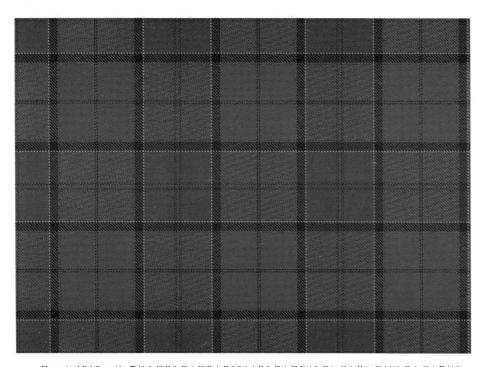

Grant, 1819 sett: **R**/16 DB2 R4 DB4 R256 LB2 R4 DB42 R6 G4 R6 G178 R4 G4 **R/12**

Grant, early 18th century fragment from Glenmorriston: **R/12** A8 B24 R22 MB24 DT8 **R/6**

Grant, Hunting—the clan wears the Black Watch tartan due to their early association with the regiment: **B/24** K4 B4 K4 B4 K20 G24 K6 G24 K20 B22 K4 **B/4**

Grant "Champion," from a portrait of Alistair Mor Grant, early eighteenth century: **G/56** Y4 G40 K4 Y56 K4 R24 Y8 **R/56**

22

Gray: Claret/6 N66 G20 Claret6 G6 Claret6 G6 Claret16 N20 **Claret/6**

Greer: W/8 R24 B20 LightTurquoise6 N6 LTurquoise6 B6 **LTurquoise/32**

Greene B/12 R8 B48 W6 K12 G36 Y8 G4 Y4 **G/8**

"Greyhound Grenadiers" Pipe Band: RoyalB/36 K28 N20 R4 N20 K4 **N/8**

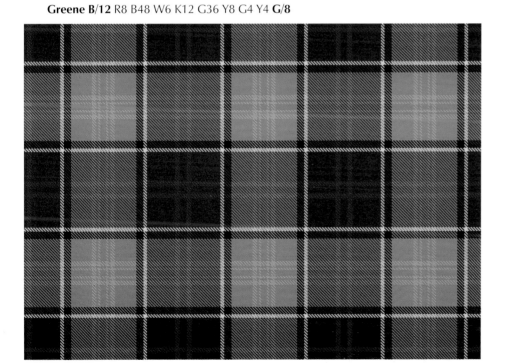

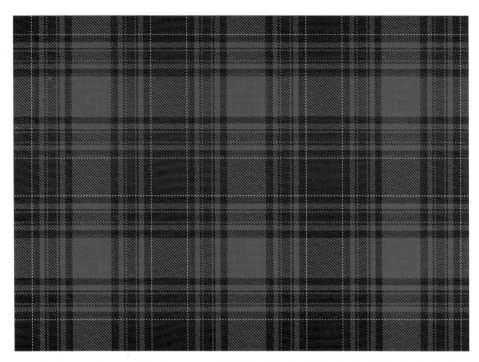

Gudbransdalen District, Norway: **R/168** W4 R12 N24 G24 R8 LT4 G8 R40 G8 LT4 R8 G24 LT24 R12 **G/176**

Gunn—reproduction colors

Gunn—weathered colors

Gunn: R/8 G48 K48 G4 B48 **G/8**

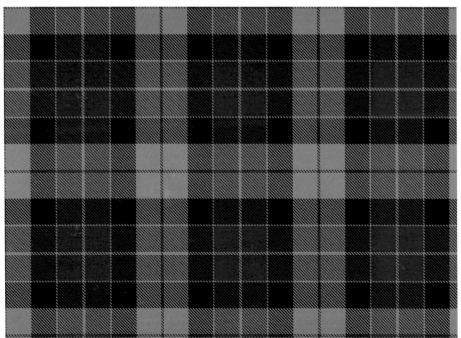

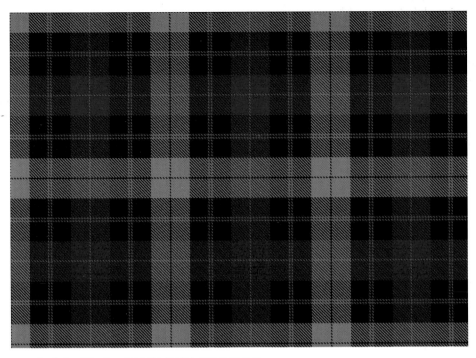

Guthrie: K/4 G48 K48 R4 K4 R4 K48 B48 **R/4**

Guthrie—reproduction colors

Hackston: R/56 W4 K24 Y6 R24 Y6 R24 **G/12**

Haig: W/12 K12 W12 K12 W12 K12 W12 K12 W121 K12 W12 K12 W12 **B/12**

25

Hakata "A", 18th century Japanese costume: B/4 W12 T24 W96 B16 **LT/8**

Hakata "B", 18th century Japanese costume: B/16 LT8 B4 T20 G4 T8 **Gold/8**

Hakata "C", 18th century Japanese costume: R/12 K2 Blue-Grey48 **K/36**

Hall: G/32 R4 B8 R4 G32 R4 B8 R4 G32 R4 **Y/4**

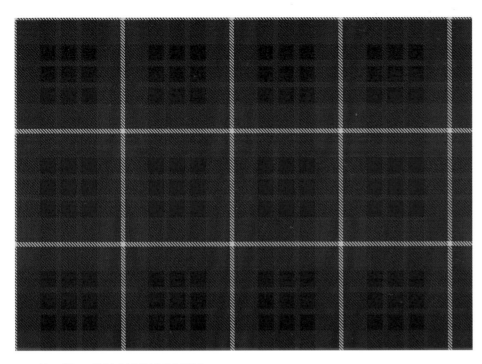

Hamilton: W/4 R18 B12 R4 **B/12**

Hamilton of Brandon: Y/12 K4 G28 N4 K28 **LT/64**

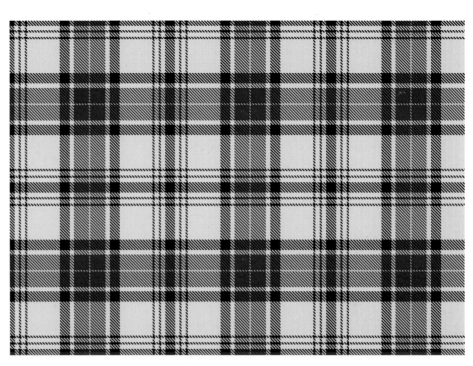

Hanna / Hannay: K/18 W8 K4 W8 K4 W60 K18 W8 B20 **Y/4**

Harkness: B/20 R4 W4 R32 G12 R2 G4 R2 G6 **R/12**

Harkness, Hunting, as woven by D.C. Dalgliesh Co.: G/32 W4 B42 G18 Y4 G10 R4 G8 **B/20**

Harkness, Hunting: G/32 B4 W4 B42 G18 Y4 G10 R4 G8 **B/20**

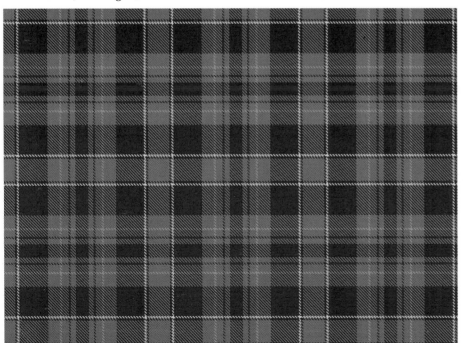

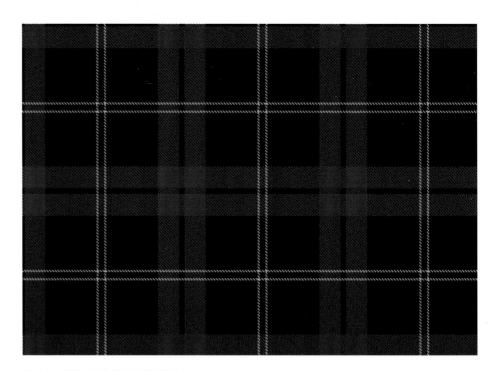

Harvie: K/16 R52 K128 Y6 **K/16**

Hay: W/4 R4 K4 R4 G4 R40 G12 R4 G4 R4 G24 Y4 G4 **R/4**

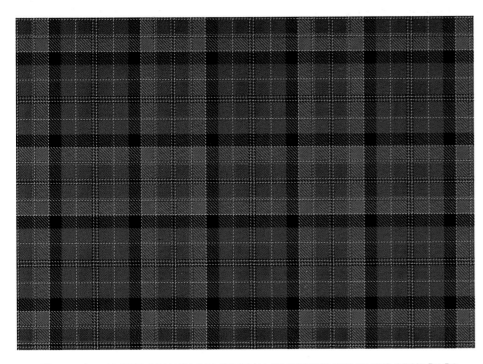

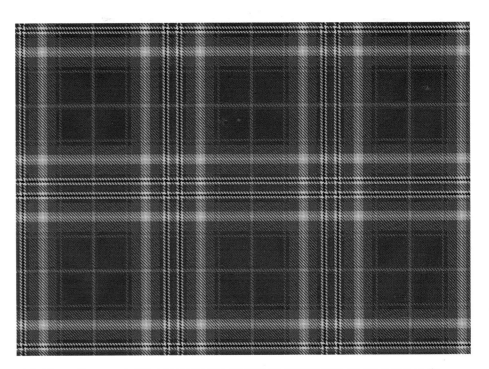

Hay, early sett: K/12 R4 Y4 K4 R64 G8 R4 Y4 R8 G60 W4 K60 R4 B60 R8 Y4 R4 B8 R64 K8 Y4 R4 **K/12**

Hebridean Tartan from South Uist (non-repeating): B/36 R4 G4 R2 Y2 G2 R40 B4 R4 G6 R4 B34 R4 W2 G6 R48 G4 R4 **...**

Hebridean, Unnamed: B/6 R4 W4 K4 W4 R6 G16 Y6 W4 Y6 G16 R6 G4 R48 B4 **N/6**

Hebridean, Unnamed: K/8 R4 B48 W4 DG28 **K/24**

Hebridean, Unnamed: B/30 R16 B4 R14 W2 G60 R4 B46 W2 R46 W2 B12 R4 G4 R4 **B/24**

Highfield: B/20 K4 G4 R4 G4 K4 W4 K4 W8 K2 **W/4**

Henderson: Y/4 K12 G8 K4 G32 B4 G12 B12 **W/4**

Highfield, Hunting: B/20 K4 G4 R4 G4 K4 DT4 K4 T8 K2 **LT/4**

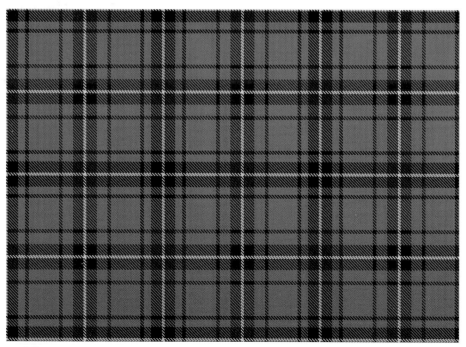

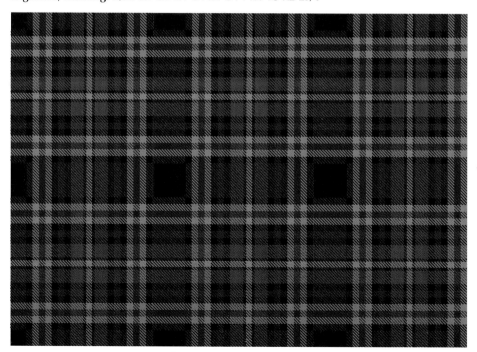

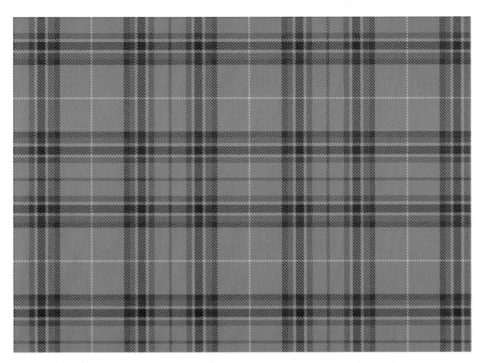

Highland District, Version 1: P/6 G28 P12 Y6 B16 Y6 P12 C12 G60 **W/4**

Highland District, Version 2: P/6 G28 LP12 LT6 B16 LT6 LP12 DT12 B60 **W/2**

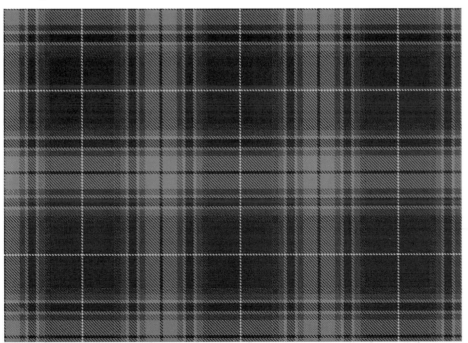

Highland Park, Texas, High School Pipe Band: Y/82 W4 Y8 W8 K8 W4 K38 W4 K8 W8 K8 W4 **K/36**

Hislop: R/6 K36 Y6 K36 G36 B36 K4 **W/8**

Hislop, Hunting: G/4 6 K4 B2 K4 B6 Y2 G6 K4 G4 K12 G4 K12 G4 K4 G48 R4 **G/8**

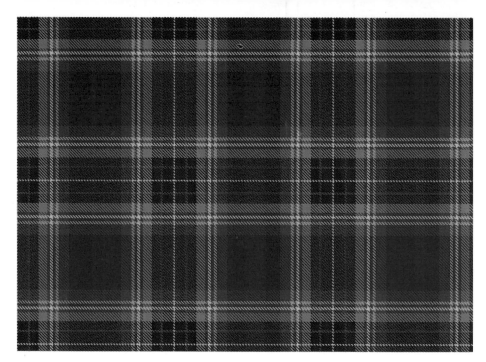

Holyrood: DB/96 SableB20 Y6 SB6 W6 SB6 G16 T16 SB4 T20 **W4**

Hogarth of Firhill: LB/8 G26 Y4 K56 **B/6**

Home: LB/6 G4 LB48 K16 R4 K4 R4 **K/36**

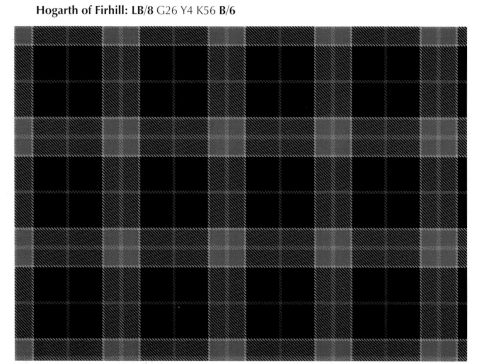

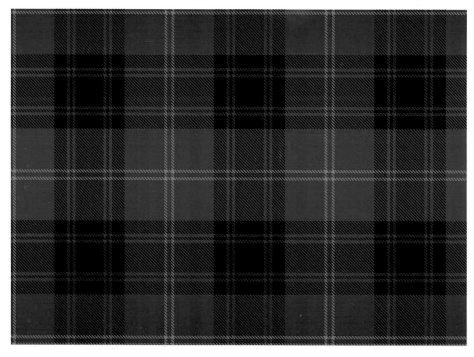

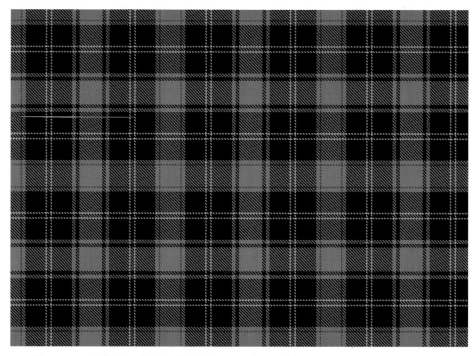

Hopetoun: G/44 B4 G8 K44 Y4 K8 Y4 K44 G8 K8 **G/52**

Hope-Vere: LB/8 G6 K14 B32 K4 Y4 K14 Y4 K4 B32 K14 G6 K4 LB6 K4 **G/36**

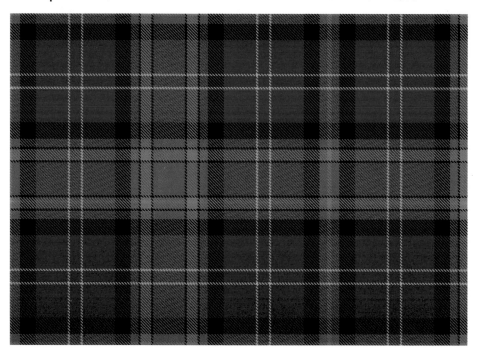

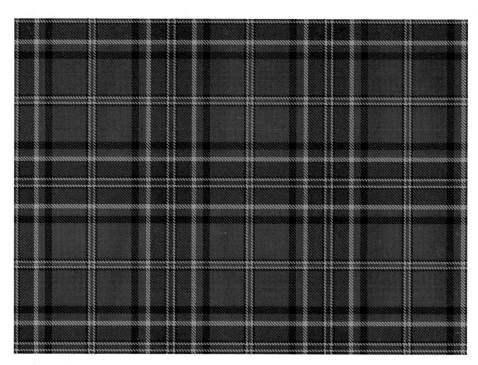

Hudson: B/8 A4 K4 B24 A8 R12 K12 R56 K4 A4 **R/6**

Hudson, Hunting: B/8 A4 K4 B24 A8 G12 K12 G56 K4 A4 **G/6**

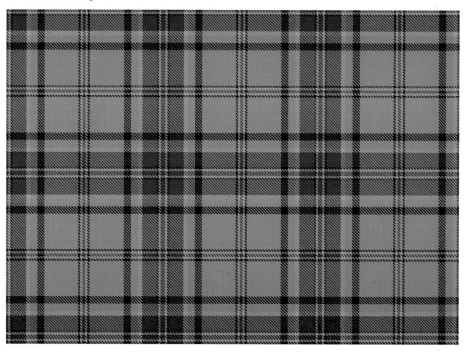

33

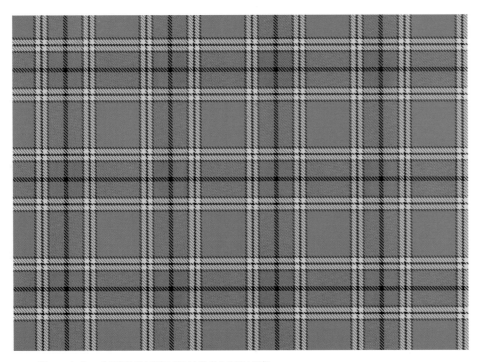

Humphries: **LG/72** R4 W8 K4 W8 R4 LT24 **K/8**

Hunter: **W/4** B32 R4 K32 G32 **K/4**

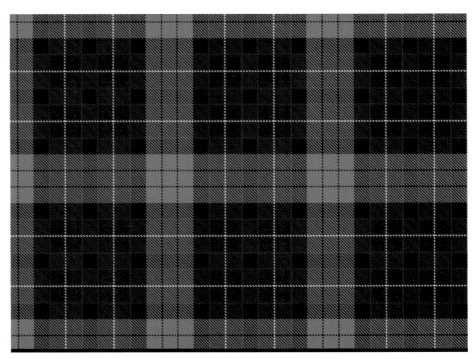

Hunter, "Telfer Dunbar's Fancy"—J.C. Thompson collection: **G/32** K4 G32 K32 R4 B32 W4 B32 R4 **K/32**

Hunter, 1819—reproduction colors: **W/4** R16 W4 K30 W4 A10 W4 R40 A4 R8 A4 R40 A6 Y6 R4 W4 R4 Y6 A6 T40 W4 R64 W4 T40 W4 A10 W4 T8 K30 W4 Q10 W4 R16 **W/4**

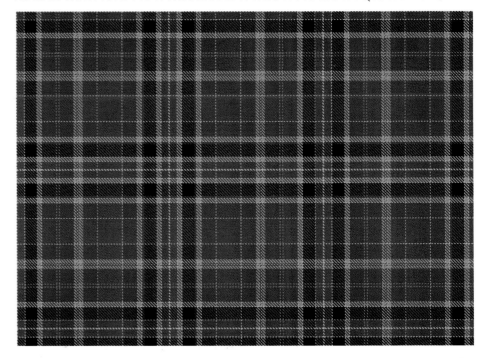

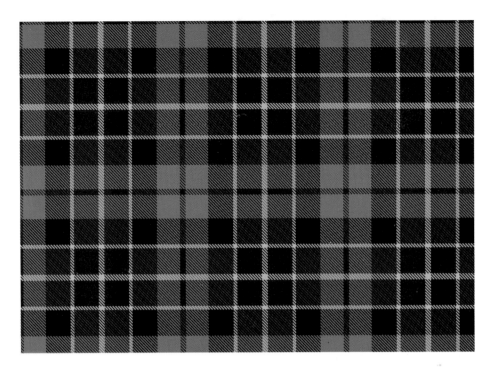

Hunter, Wilson's sett: W/4 R20 W4 K44 W4 B12 W4 DG48 LG4 DG8 LG4 DG48 LG8 Y8 R4 W4 R4 Y8 LG8 DG48 W4 R76 W4 DG48 W4 B12 W4 LG8 K40 W4 B12 W4 R20 **W/4**

Huntly District: G/16 R4 G16 R24 G4 R6 G4 R24 W4 R6 Y4 B24 R6 B24 Y4 R6 W4 R24 B4 R4 B4 R4 B4 R24 B4 R4 B4 R4 B4 R24 G16 R4 **G/16**

Hurd / Herd: B/6 G24 K26 W4 B26 **W/6**

Hynde: G/56 R4 G56 R14 W4 R14 W4 R14 K10 P8 **W/4**

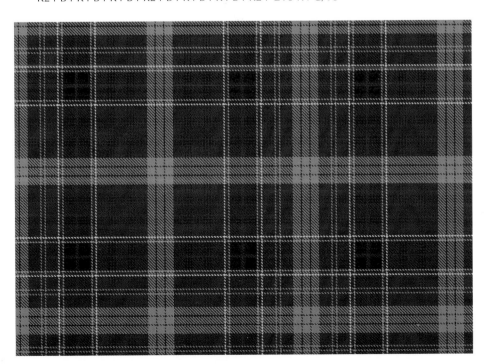

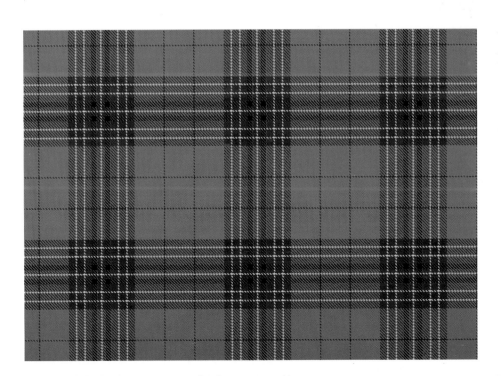

Hyndman: B/8 R4 B6 R10 B24 G12 LT4 G4 K4 B18 R10 B4 R6 **W/6**

Hyslop: G/4 B6 K4 B2 K4 B6 Y2 G6 K4 G4 K12 G4 K12 G4 K4 G48 R4 **G/8**

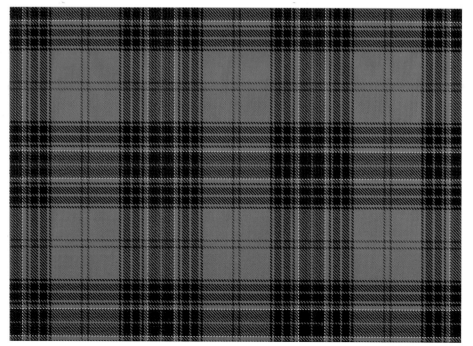

Idaho State Tartan: LB/24 R4 LB4 R4 LB4 G20 W24 Y6 W24 G20 LB24 R4 **LB/4**

Ikelman: R/32 G4 R6 G4 R26 B24 W4 B24 R26 K26 R4 **Y/4**

36

Indiana "Cardinal" State Tartan: B/32 Y4 G48 R40 T8 R24 T8 **R/16**

Inglis / Ingles: W/8 G48 B20 R6 B24 **Y/8**

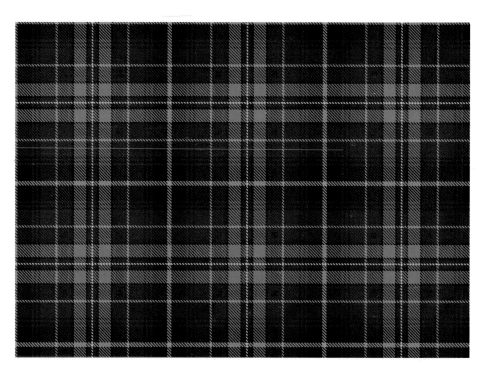

Innes: A/14 K48 R8 K8 R8 K8 R48 Y8 R12 B24 R12 K8 G40 K8 R12 **W/8**

Innes of Cowie: B/2 K12 R2 K2 R2 K2 R12 W2 R4 G6 R4 K2 G10 K2 R4 G6 R4 W2 R12 K2 R2 K2 R2 K12 **G/2**

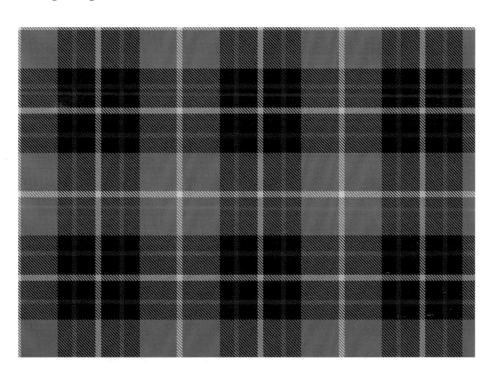

Innes of Edingight: A/4 K12 A2 G14 K2 **G/14**

Inverness District, alternative sett: R/60 Y8 B12 Y8 K28 W8 K24 **R/156**

Inverness District: R/144 B12 W4 B22 G4 K4 G4 **R/36**

Irvine of Drum: W/6 B6 K6 B42 **G/96**

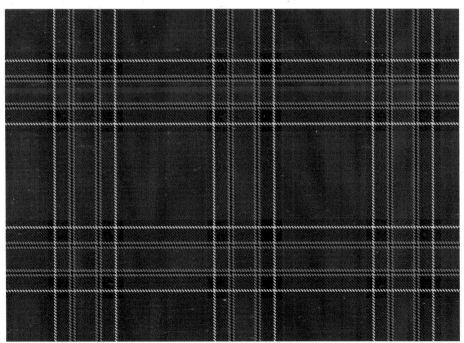

Irving of Bonshaw Tower: R/4 G6 B4 G28 B28 **W/4**

Irving of Glentulchan: R/6 G54 B54 K6 B6 **W/6**

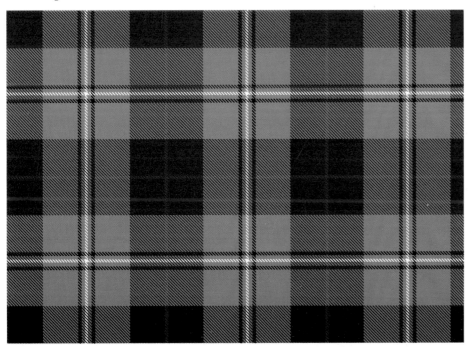

Isle of Man: R/4 A22 T4 W3 G7 Y2 G4 W2 G9 P6 Y2 P4 **W/4**

Isle of Skye

Jacobite, signaling adherence to the Stuart cause in the civil wars: W/4 R8 B8 W4 Orange32 W4 B8 R8 W4 R8 B8 W4 G32 W4 B8 R8 **W/8**
Jacobite relic, a riding cloak worn by Prince Charles: W/4 R12 Y8 G48 Y16 K8 Y16 G12 **R/48**

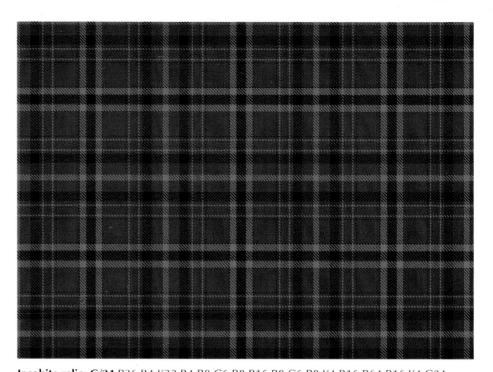

Jacobite relic: G/24 R36 B4 K32 B4 R8 G6 R8 B16 R8 G6 R8 K4 B16 R64 B16 K4 G24 R4 **K/32**
Jacobite relic, a coat worn by Prince Charles: G/12 R4 G4 R48 A2 B2 R4 B24 R4 A2 R4 G48 **R/4**

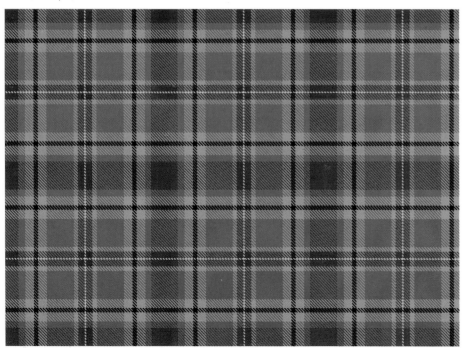

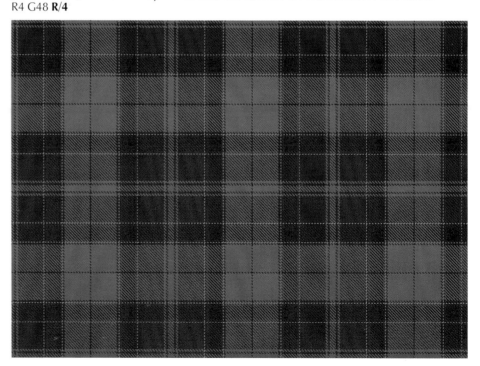

Jacobite relic, from a coat said to have been worn at the battle of Culloden, 1746:
R/12 W4 K80 W4 A28 G28 Y6 W4 G12 P12 Y4 A12 P60 R24 **W/4**

Jacobite relic, Carmichael collection: C/24 K8 C12 W14 C34 K24 C6 DY22 Y14 W4
K6 W4 Y14 C16 K8 W6 A6 **W/4**

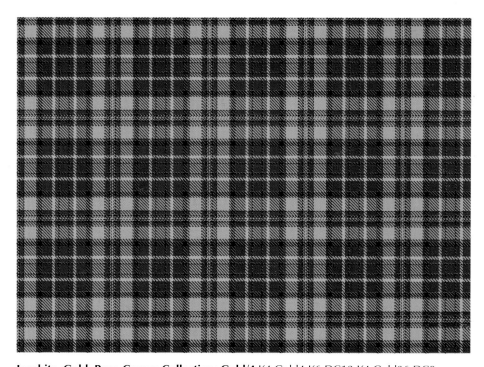

Jacobite, Gold, Ross-Craven Collection: Gold/4 K4 Gold4 K6 DC12 K4 Gold36 DC8
K14 DC30 W10 DC12 K6 **DC/28**

Jacobite, Dress: W/2 A4 R4 K6 R12 Y12 W2 K4 W2 Y12 LY24 R8 K24 R32 W14 R12
K12 **R/18**

Jahore Regiment: B/40 K10 B36 Y52 **K/112**

James: A/10 B24 Y4 G50 Y4 K24 **R/10**

Jardine: R/52 K4 R6 K4 R6 K18 W4 B40 W4 K6 G64 **K/6**

Jardine, "Old": DT/36 MT36 DDB36 R4 A4 MT36 LN4 R4...

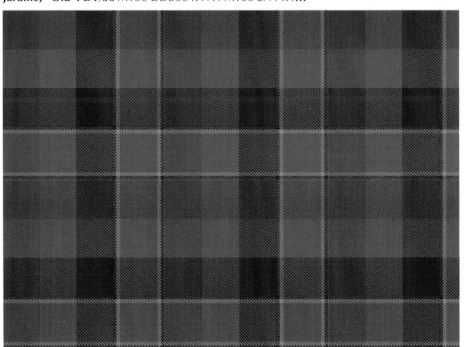

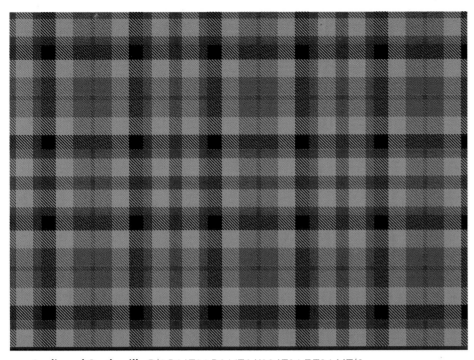

Jardine of Castlemilk: R/6 B6 LT24 B6 MT6 K20 LT24 DT24 **MT/6**

Johnston(e): K/4 B4 K4 B48 G48 K4 G4 **Y/4**

Johnston(e)—reproduction colors

Johnston(e), Dress: **K/6** B6 K6 B36 G40 K6 G6 Y6 G6 K6 G40 W6 B6 W6 B6 W24 B6 **W/6**

Johnston, color variation (used by the Atlas Textile Co., N. Wales, Pennsylvania, c. 1945-65): R/4 K4 R4 K48 R48 K4 R4 **W/4**

Johnston(e), *Clan Originaux* **version: B/4** K4 B4 K4 B48 G48 K4 G4 **Y/4**

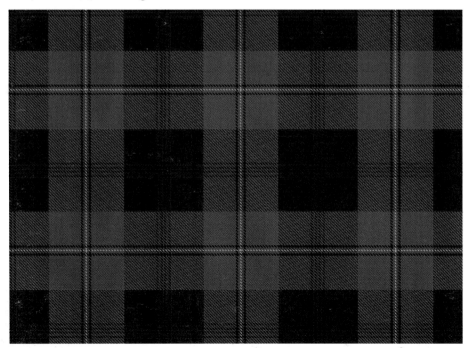

Jones: R/8 W2 LG12 G50 K16 B30 **W/4**

Jubilee: G/6 A24 G8 A12 G44 R6 G44 A48 G6 A48 G44 Y6 G44 A12 G8 A24 **G/6**

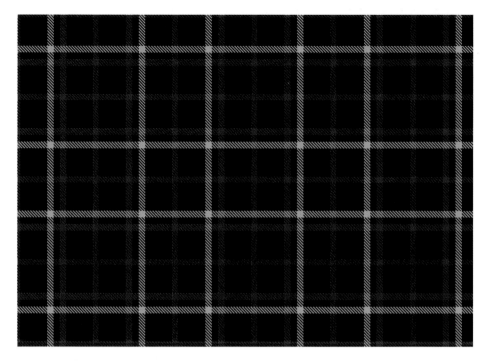

Justus / Justice: B/12 K48 Y12 K12 R12 K48 **B/12**

Kennedy: **R/4** G48 B8 K6 B6 K6 B6 K6 B8 G24 M4 G4 M4 G6 Y4 G4 **K/4**

Keith: K/4 G18 B8 K8 **B/8**

Kennedy—reproduction colors

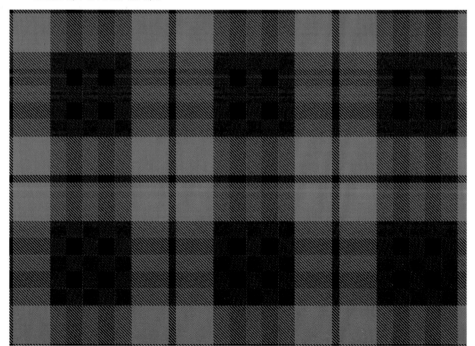

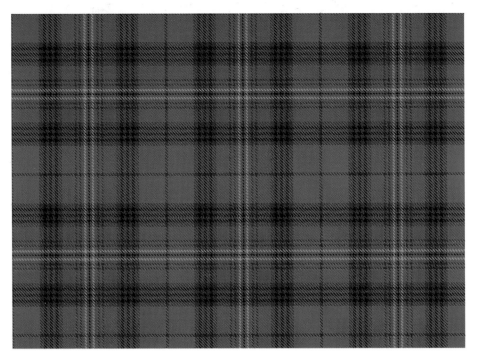

Kennedy, color variation: R/6 DG18 T8 K6 T6 K6 T6 K6 T8 DG24 R4 DG4 R4 DG6 Y4 DG4 **K/4**

Kennedy—the Irish family: K/4 RoyalB8 K26 R6 K10 Y4 K4 Y4 K16 RB16 K4 RB8 **W/4**

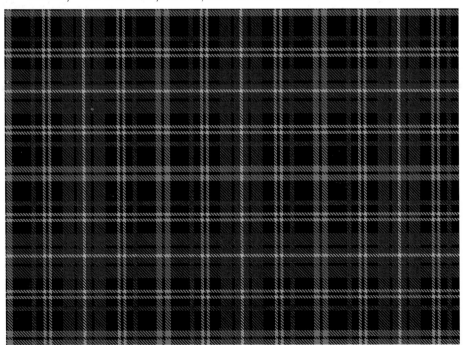

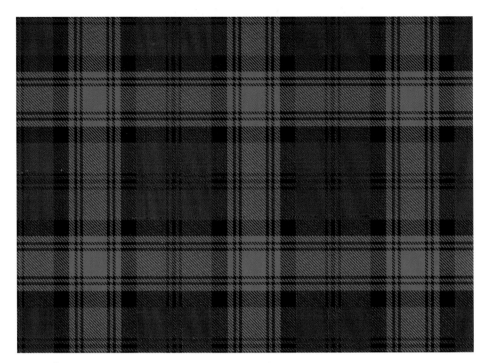

Kerr: K/6 DR4 K4 DR38 K20 DG8 K4 DG4 K4 **DG/32**

Kerr, Hunting: K/6 B4 K4 B38 K20 G8 K4 G4 K4 **G/32**

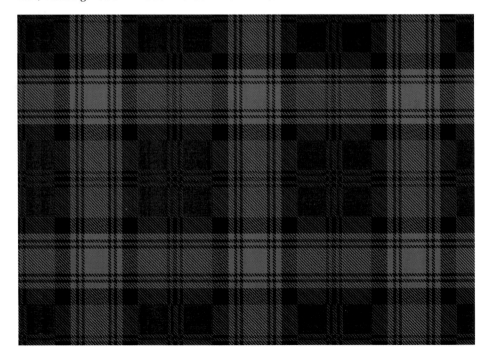

Kidd, as woven by Lochcarron Mills: R/16 A6 R16 G24 Y4 K36 A16 K4 A4 K4 A16 R20 W6 K6 **R/4**

Kiernan: W/4 G36 R4 K8 R4 K4 R4 K12 G8 **W/4**

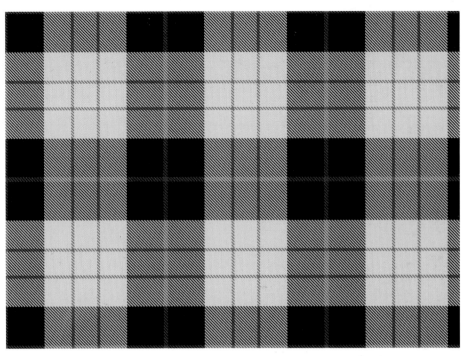

Kierson: R/6 K44 W32 DG4 **W/28**

Kile / Kyle: DDB/36 R4 DDB6 R20 DDB12 R10 DDB12 **R/108**

King George VI: W/4 R4 K4 R12 G12 K4 B4 K4 B4 K4 Y4 K6 G68 **R/4**

King George VI, yellow pivot: R/4 G60 K4 Y4 K4 B4 K4 B4 K4 G12 R12 G4 R4 **Y/4**

Kinnoull, Wilson's 1819 "short count": G/56 R12 G46 R50 G8 R20 G8 R50 W6 R20 A62 R12 A62 R20 W6 R50 K4 R4 K8 R4 K4 R50 K4 R4 K8 R4 K4 R50 G46 R12 **G/56**

Kinross Family: Orange/72 W2 A12 W2 DB16 R8 DB8 R48 BB8 O16 W2 A12 W2 Y36 O12 DB8 O12 Y36 W2 A12 W2 Y16 DB8 O48 DB8 O8 DB16 **W/8**

48

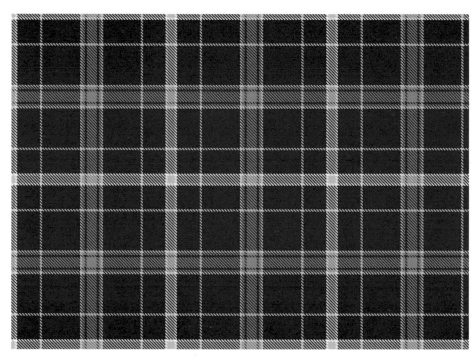

Knox: LB/12 W4 B36 Y4 B36 Y4 DB24 Y4 G4 R4 **G/16**

Lamont: B/12 K4 B4 K4 B4 K16 G16 W4 G16 K16 B16 K4 **B/4**

Lanark District: A/4 R20 G12 R4 B12 **C/4**

Largs District: B/4 R4 DB44 W6 DB5 Y4 DB3 Y8 DB3 Y16 B4 R24 **W/4**

Lasting Sett (No one knows why it is called by this name): W/4 R6 A4 R6 W8 R38 W4 DP14 W4 DP14 W4 G38 W4 Y8 W4 DP8 W4 Y8 W4 A12 W4 DP14 **W/16**
"Latin," a tartan reconstructed by Ross-Craven from the Latin description of the Lochaber men in 1689: **B/6** Y18 B6 Y18 B40 **R/6**

Lauder: R/4 G30 K8 G6 B16 **G/6**

Law of Atholl: B/20 R6 B6 R12 B52 G24 R12 G4 R6 G12 **Y/4**

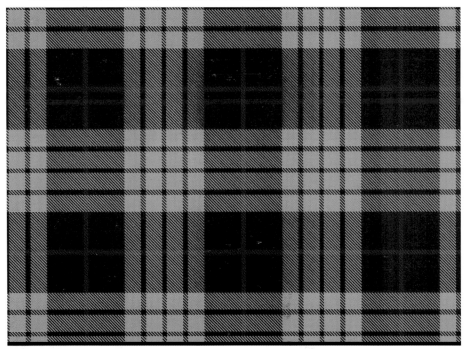

Lawers: R/112 K4 B12 K4 G12 K4 **R/112**

Laxey Manx: LB/8 G24 Y4 DP12 LB40 **W/4**

Lawless / Lawliss: DB/40 G4 DB4 G4 DB4 G8 R48 G4 **R/8**

Leach: LB/4 R12 G48 R4 G8 R4 K20 LB8 R48 K6 R6 **K/12**

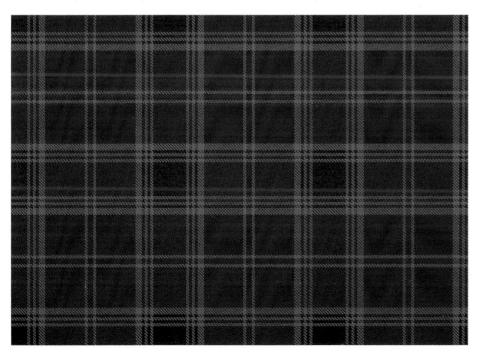

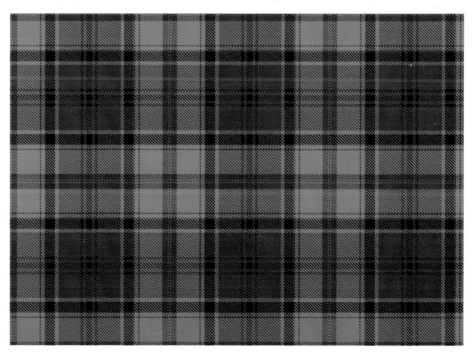

Leask: G/10 R6 W4 R6 K4 R68 G32 Y4 G8 Y4 G32 R4 G8 **Y/8**

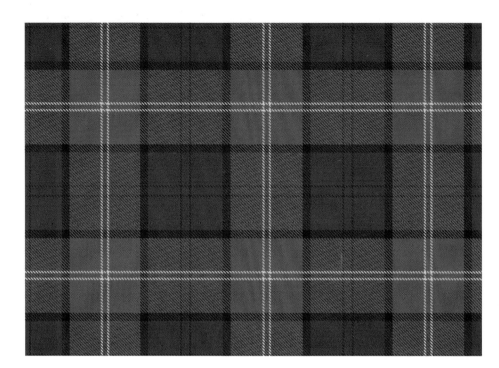

Leckie: R/12 B4 R48 C12 G48 W4 **G/8**

"Leatherneck," a tartan for the U.S. Marine Corps: G/80 R6 G8 R8 G24 B64 Y8 **R/6**

Ledford: DG/32 MN16 **Y/4**

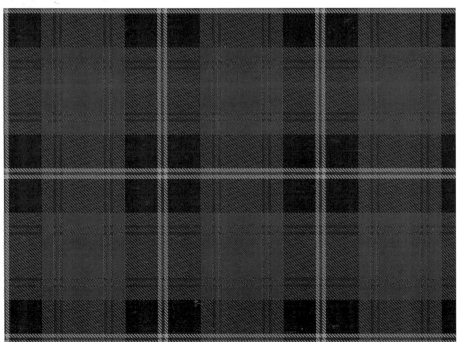

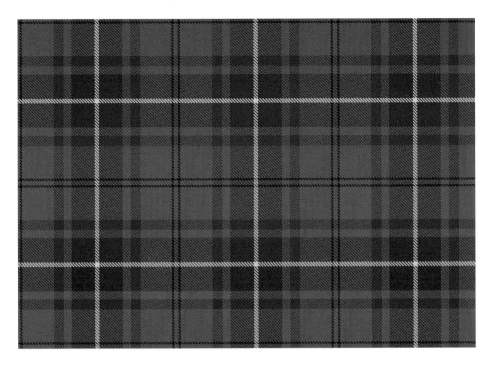

Lee: G/4 K2 G24 R8 G6 B18 **W/4**

Leighton: R/8 DT28 T16 DT20 DG36 DT20 Y4 **DT/20**

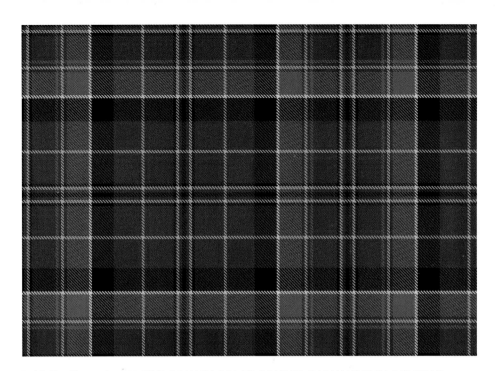

Leith Family, early sett: K/12 R4 Y4 K4 R64 G8 R4 Y4 R8 G60 W4 K60 R4 B60 R8 Y4 R4 B8 R64 K8 Y4 R4 **K/12**

Leith Family (Hay and Leith): K/6 R2 Y2 K4 R32 G4 R2 Y2 R4 G30 W2 K30 R4 P30 R4 Y2 R2 P4 R32 K4 Y2 R2 **K/6**

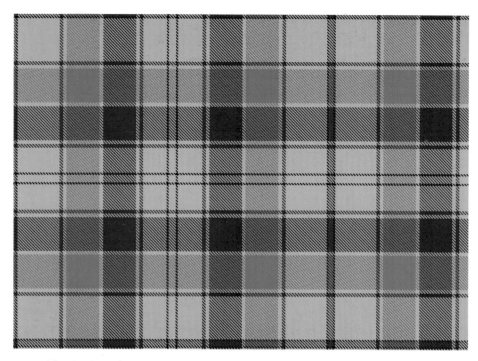

Leith District: R/8 K4 LB60 B6 LB6 G48 LB6 B48 LB6 B6 LB36 K4 **LB/12**

Lendrum: R/36 K4 R28 **K/48**

Lennie Family: G/4 P16 K18 A4 G20 **K/4**

Lennox District and Family: R/8 DR4 R40 DR8 G40 W4 **G/8**

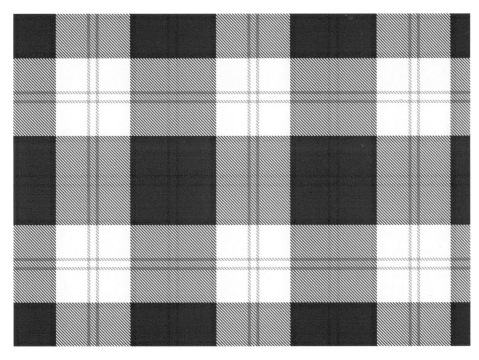

Lennox, Dress: R/8 DR4 R40 GR8 W40 G4 **W/8**

Leonard Family: B/36 K40 B20 **K/60**

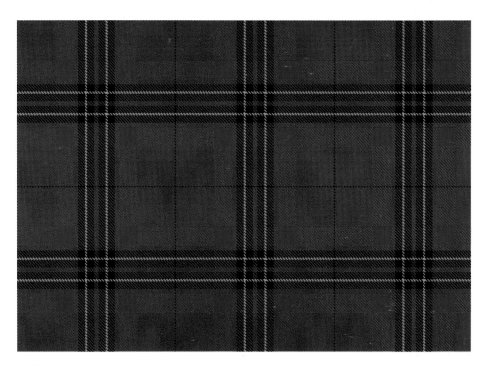

Leslie, "Red": **K/4** R64 B32 R8 K12 Y4 K12 **R/8**

Leslie, Hunting: **R/4** B16 K16 W2 G16 **K/4**

Lindsay: **DC/6** B4 DC48 B16 K4 B4 K4 B4 **K/40**

Lindsay—weathered colors

Lions International: **LP/60** A2 K2 P2 Y2 LP10 W4 Y12 LP10 K2 A6 LP6 W2 A2 W2 LP6 A4 LP4 K4 **W/8**

Little: **K/16** W16 K16 W16 K16 R32 K8 R32 K32 **Y/8**

Livingstone: R/16 G4 R40 G32 R8 K4 R4 K4 R8 **G/24**

Livingstone, Dress: Y/8 K4 W8 K8 W6 K8 W6 K6 W40 K4 Y6 K4 W6 K6 W6 **B/108**

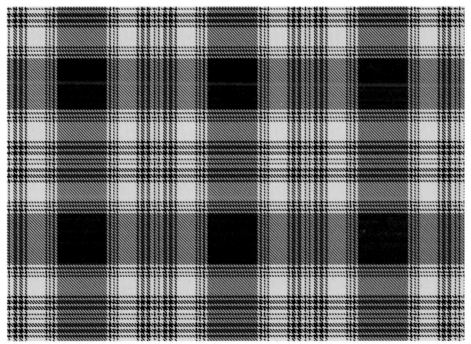

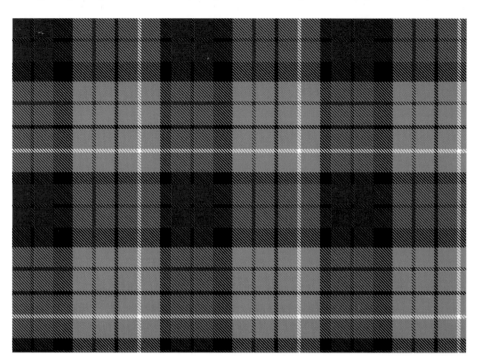

Lloyd of Dolobran, McGregor-Hastie collection: B/20 K4 B20 K20 G20 R4 G20 K4 G20 W4 G20 K12 ...

Lobban: B/4 R4 B4 R4 B24 K18 G24 R4 G4 **Y/4**

Loch Laggan District: G/12 K8 G144 R4 G16 **R/28**

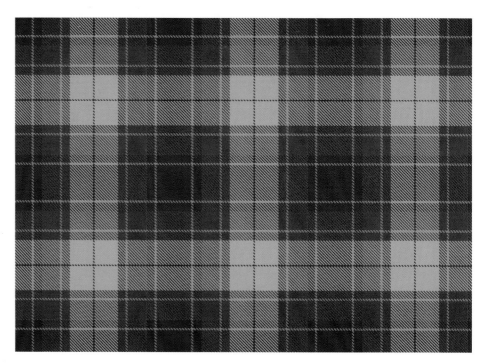

Loch Rannoch District: DT/52 G4 DT12 T28 G4 T12 Y36 **K/4**

Loch Leven District: B/4 W10 LB8 B22 G26 **B/4**

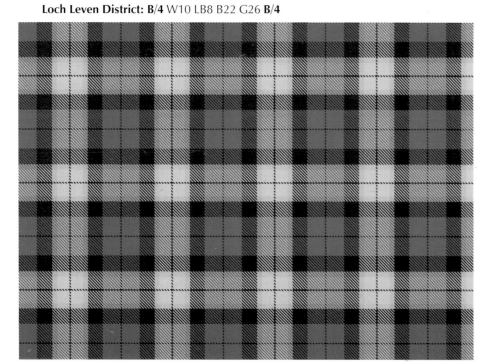

Lochaber, after Christian Heskith: K/8 A4 K80 Y6 K240 Y6 **K/16**

Lochaber District—weathered colors

Lochaber District, Wilson's 1797 sett: MB/8 A4 MB64 R4 MB140 R4 **MB/12**

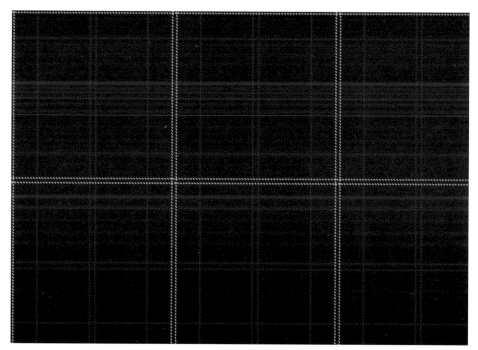

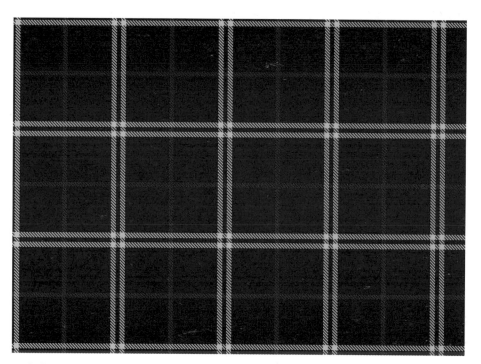

Lochaber: DB/4 A4 DB32 **R/4**

Lochaber, Ingles Buchan's sett: Greenish T12 K4 R10 K4 G-T44 K44 R8 N44 LN8 **G-T/12**

59

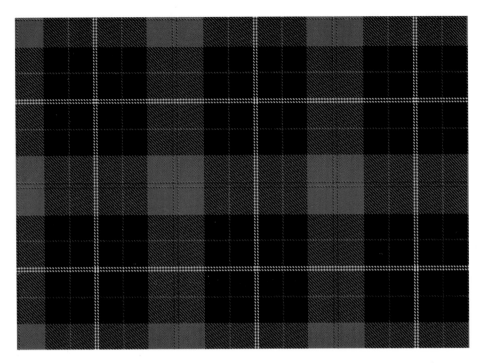

Lochaber, W. Highland Museum collection: DG/10 R4 G68 K64 R4 K64 W4 **K/6**

Lochcarron, Dress: R/6 B20 LB6 B4 LB4 B4 R6 K10 R4 K10 R44 G4 R6 **G/4**

Lochcarron, Hunting: G/6 B20 GrayB6 B4 GrayB4 B4 G6 K10 G4 K10 G44 R4 G6 **R/4**

Lochiel: G/16 R6 Y4 K4 R68 LG6 R8 **LG/4**

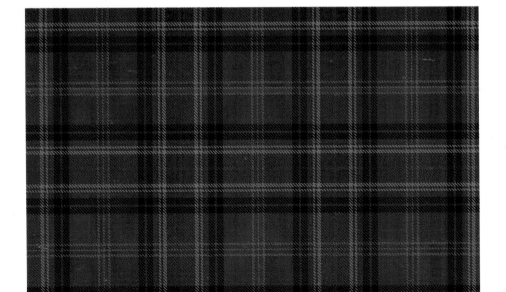

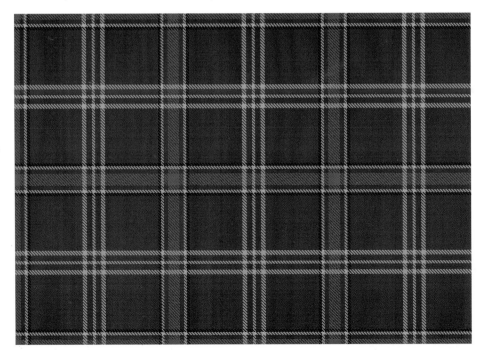

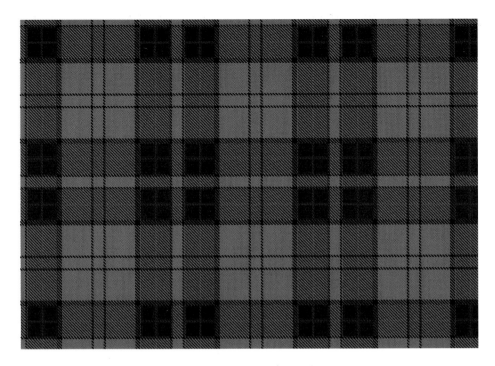

Lockhart: G/24 K6 B32 R4 B32 K12 G64 K6 **G/24**

Loevenstein Castle #1—a tartan painted on a figure of a Scottish mercenary c. 1740-50 on a wall in Loevenstein Castle, the Netherlands: **K/14** W4 R8 K6 **R/40**

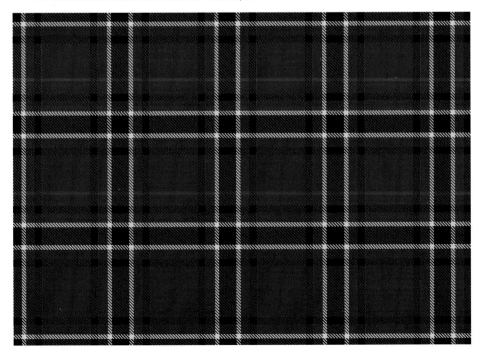

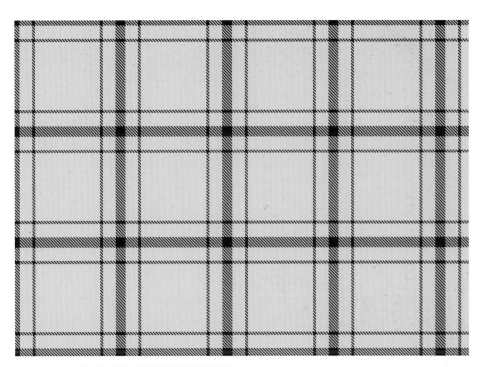

Loevenstein Castle #2: B/12 W16 B4 **W/80**

Loevenstein Castle #3: B/80 R2 W8 R4 B16 **W/48**

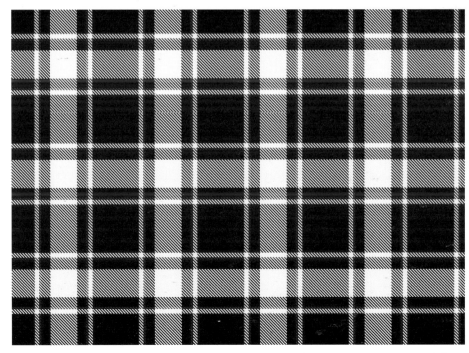

Logan: B/40 R12 B4 R12 G40 R12 **G/4**

Logan, *Clan Originaux* **version: B/18** R6 B18 R6 K18 R4 W4 **G/80**

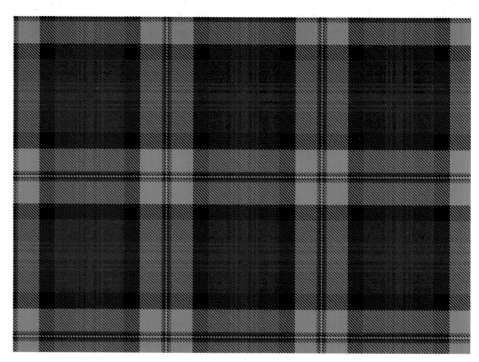

Logan / MacLennan: B/24 R8 B26 R8 K24 R8 W6 **G/110**

London Caledonian Games Association: R/18 B4 R42 A4 R4 B16 R4 G4 R4 G34 R4 B4 **R/16**

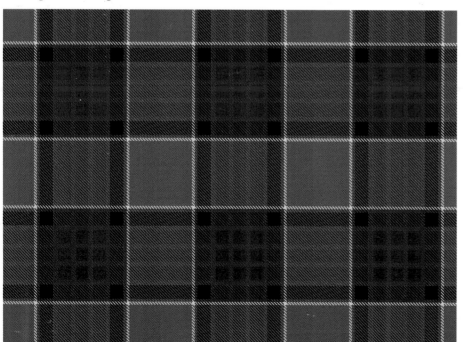

Lord Loudoun's Highlanders: R/8 K4 B48 K40 G40 **Y/6**

Lorne District: B/8 K4 DG32 K4 DG4 K4 DG4 K32 B4 K4 B4 K4 B32 K4 **DG/8**

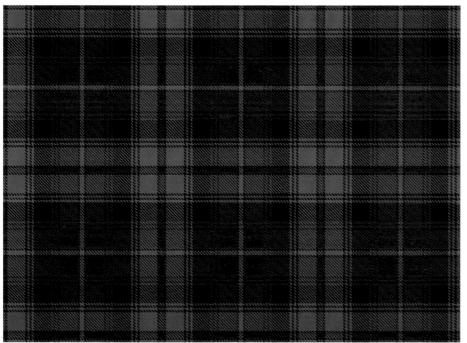

Loton: R/8 G68 B8 G8 **R/24**

Lumsden: R/4 B28 R8 W4 R20 G4 R10 G4 R20 G12 R8 G12 R8 G8 Y4 G8 R8 G16 W4 **G/16**

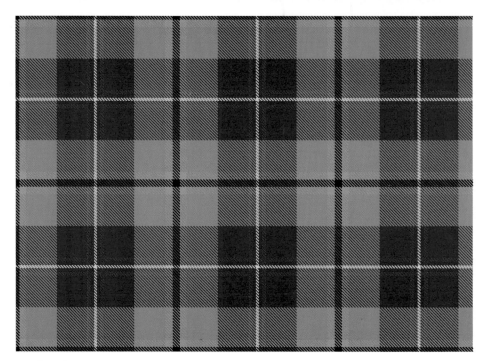

Lumsden of Boghead: G/72 R8 G62 R62 G8 R16 G8 R62 B62 R8 B62 R62 B4 R4 B8 R4 B4 **K/8**

Lundy: K/8 LB8 G32 B32 R4 B4 **W/4**

Lumsden of Kintore: G/4 R24 G16 R4 G4 R4 B16 R24 **B/4**

Lynch: R/12 LB8 R4 LB72 LG4 **LB/8**

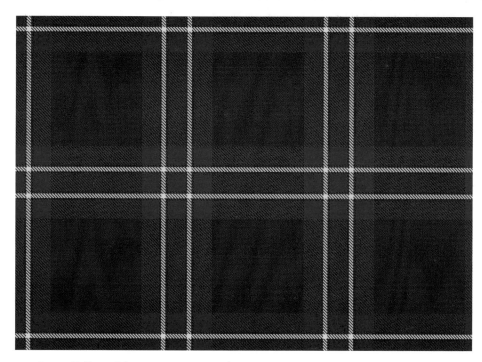

Lyons College: B/32 R4 W8 R4 B32 **R/160**

Lyons: B/32 K4 B4 K4 B4 K20 G24 W2 B4 W2 G24 K20 B22 K4 **B/4**

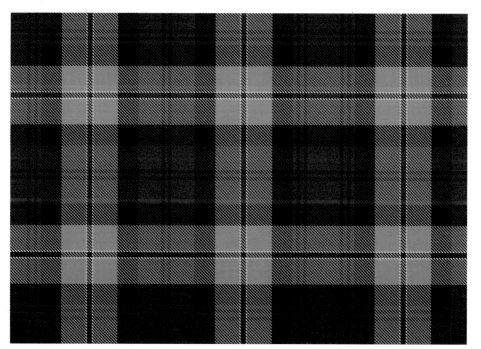

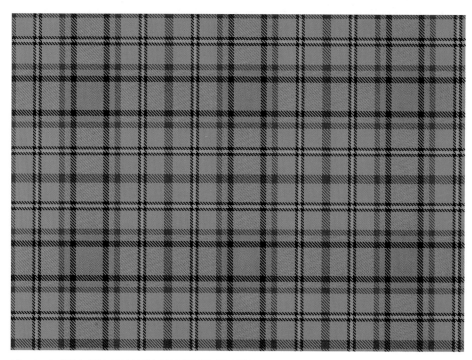

MacAart: R/12 G24 K4 Y4 K4 G24 R8 T8 K8 **T/36**
MacAlister, as woven by Lochcarron Mills: R/12 W4 R4 B4 R4 W4 R4 G6 R6 G6 R4 W4 R4 B6 R4 W4 R16 A4 R4 G16 R4 A4 R32 A4 R4 K16 R4 A4 R16 W4 R4 G6 R4 A4 R4 W4 R4 A4 R4 G6 **R/12**

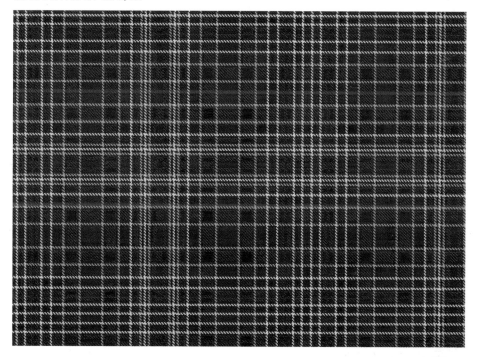

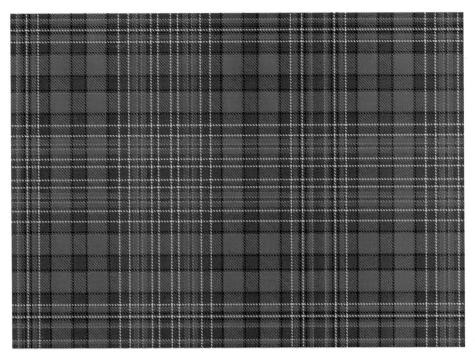

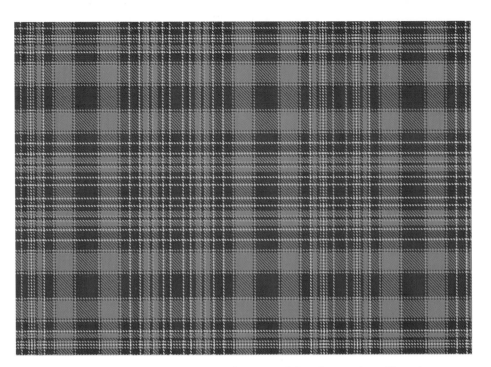

MacAlisiter, Logan's sett: B/20 R4 W4 R6 DG24 LG4 R16 LG4 DG24 R20 W4 R4 B32 R4 W4 R44 A4 R4 DG88 R4 A4 R128 A4 R4 DG88 R4 A4 R48 W4 R4 DG24 R8 A8 R8 W4 R8 A8 R8 DG24 LG4 **R/16**

MacAlister, as woven by Meyer and Mortimer, 19th century: R/48 G12 Y4 R8 Y4 G12 R12 B12 R24 A4 R4 G32 R4 A4 R48 A4 R4 G32 R4 A4 R24 G8 R4 A4 R8 A4 R4 G12 Y4 **R/16**

MacAlister, as in the Smiths' *Authenticated Tartans of the Clans and Families of Scotland*, 1850: **R/16** LG2 DG4 R4 A2 R2 W2 R2 A2 R4 DG6 R2 W2 R12 A2 R2 DG24 R2 A2 R32 A2 R2 DG24 R2 A2 R12 W2 R2 B8 R2 W2 R4 DG6 LG2 R2 LG2 DG6 R6 W2 R2 B4 R2 W2 **R/16**

MacAlister of Glenbarr: R/16 W/6 B6 R92 B4 R4 G40 R4 B4 R16 G12 R12 G12 R6 **G/40**

MacAlister of Glenbarr, old sett: W/6 R8 DB6 R100 DB4 R4 G40 R4 DB4 R16 G12 R12 G12 R8 G16 **W/6**

MacAlpine: G/8 K16 Y4 K16 G4 K4 G24 K4 G24 K4 G4 K16 W4 **K/32**

MacAlpine, "Old": G/4 K16 Y4 K16 G4 K4 G24 K4 G24 K4 G4 K16 W4 K16 …

MacArthur: Y/6 G60 K24 G12 **K/64**

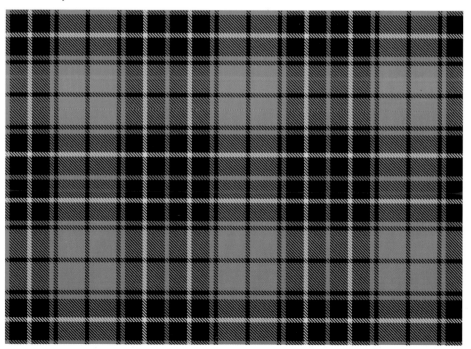

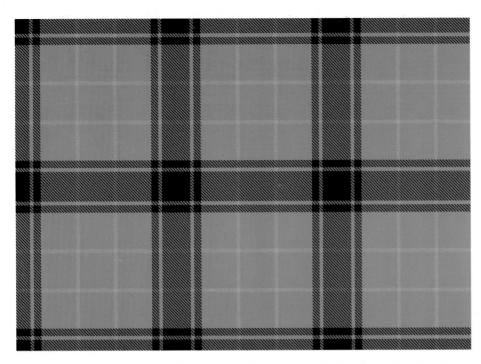

MacArthur, "Two Yellow Stripes" (Found in an early collection, but believed to be a weaver's error.): **G/36** Y4 G36 K8 G4 **K/30**

MacArthur of Milton: **G/32** B4 G4 K18 B20 **K/8**

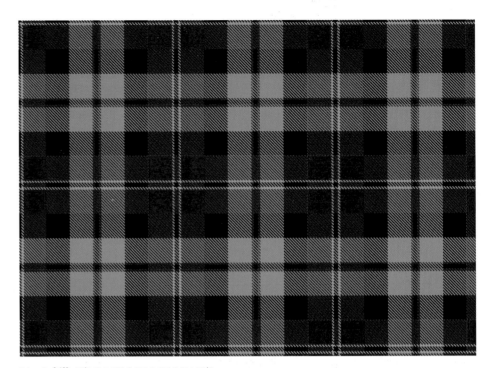

MacAskill: **K/8** R4 G36 K36 B36 Y4 **K/8**

MacAulay: **K/4** R32 G12 R6 G16 **W/4**

MacAulay, as found in the *Baronage of Angus and the Mearns*, 1856: R/192 B2 G48 B2 R20 B2 G24 K2 **W/8**

MacAulay, Hunting: G/12 K32 W4 K32 G16 K8 G24 **R/4**

MacBain / MacBean: R/96 W4 B8 LB4 W4 LB4 B8 W4 K4 G24 K4 W4 R8 DR8 G4 DR8 R8W4 **G/12**

MacBean of Tomatin: B/3 R38 B26 R10 G42 R16 **B/6**

MacBeth: B/144 Y16 K20 Y4 K4 W4 K8 G32 R24 K4 R12 **W/4**

MacBrine: K/8 R12 G16 R32 K12 B20 K4 B20 K4 G16 **Y/2**

MacBriar of Almagill and Netherwood: R/8 W4 R56 DG56 W4 R56 K4 **MT/200**

MacCainish, Alex Lumsden collection: R/4 B16 K2 G4 K2 G8 K2 G4 K2 B16 **Y/4**

MacCallum: K/4 B12 K12 G8 A4 K4 **G/16**

MacCandlish: A/12 K4 DR48 K4 DR4 K8 DR4 K24 R48 K4 **Y/4**

MacCallum of Berwick: K/4 B12 K12 G12 R4 G12 **K/12**

MacCandlish, Hunting: Y/4 K4 G48 K24 DG4 K8 DG4 K4 DG48 K4 **W/12**

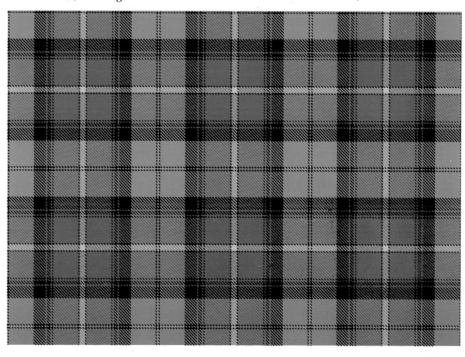

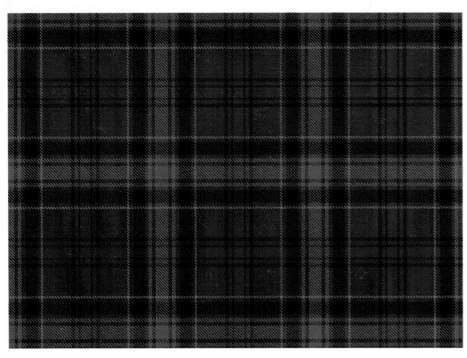

MacClintock, *Clan Originaux* **version: G/20** R6 G6 R6 K18 R6 A4 R42 K6 R6 K4 **R/16**

MacClure: K/4 R8 G8 R60 K8 R8 B16 K8 G24 R8 W4 **K/8**

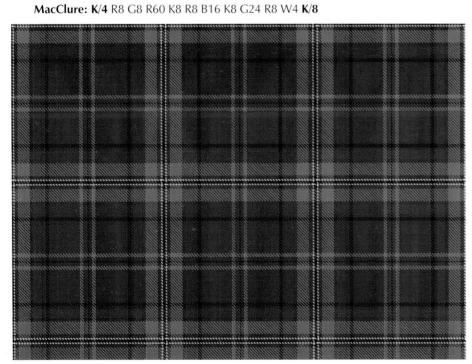

MacClure, Hunting: K/4 W2 G4 T12 G4 B8 G4 K4 G30 R4 G4 **K/2**

MacColl: G/8 R4 G4 R24 B4 R4 B6 R4 B4 R4 G16 R4 B4 **R/24**

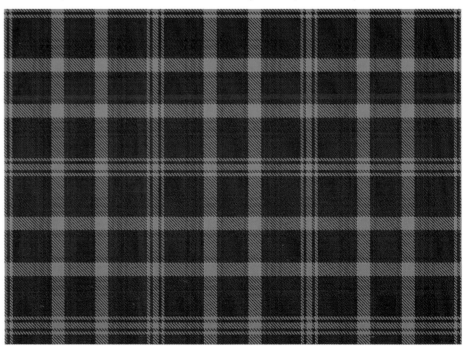

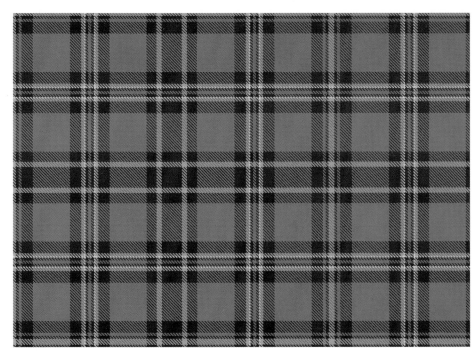

MacColl, "Old": **A/8** R4 G4 R14 G44 R14 A4 W2 R4 G4 R4 W2 A4 R14 G44 R12 A6 **R/24**

MacColl, "Old"—McGregor Hastie collection: **P/4** R4 G4 R14 G44 R14 P4 W2 R4 B4 R4 W2 P4 R14 B44 R12 P6 **R/12**

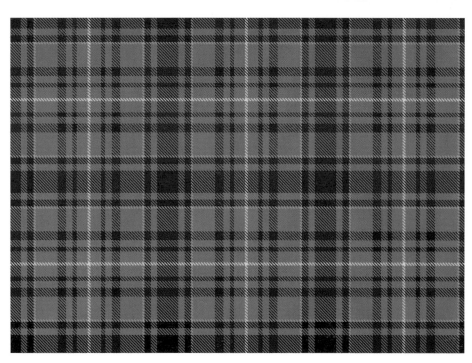

MacConnell: **B/20** G12 B12 LB4 G40 R16 G12 R8 G20 **W/6**

MacCord: **W/4** LB32 DB40 R6 LB2 R4 **G/12**

MacCormick (not MacCormack): K/6 G26 K20 R26 K4 **R**/6

MacCoul: DR/8 R72 P2 R4 G24 R24 G24 DR12 R4 DR12 B24 R8 G4 R8 G4 R4 DR4 **R**/2

MacCraig: R/16 A8 G56 R8 K56 G8 B56 R8 **G**/16

MacCreary: R/8 R8 R48 Y4 G16 B8 A6 B24 **K**/8

MacCullough: K/4 R36 G4 R10 **G/32**

MacDevitt: B/24 K4 B4 K4 B4 K20 R24 K6 R24 K20 B24 K4 **B/4**

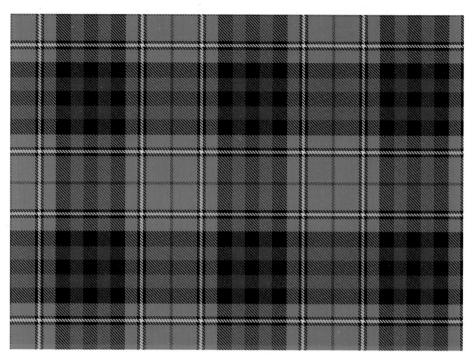

MacDiarmid / MacDermitt: R/6 G52 K6 W6 K6 G26 K32 R28 **K/30**

MacDonagh / MacDonough: K/40 G20 R12 G32 B20 G58 **R/40**

MacDonald, Clan—modern colors: DB/16 DR2 DB4 DR6 DB24 DR2 K24 DG24 DR6 DG4 DR2 **DG/16**

MacDonald, Clan—ancient colors: LB/32 LR6 LB8 LR12 LB48 LR6 K48 LG24 LR12 LG8 LR6 **LG/32**

MacDonald, Dress: G/8 R4 G4 R4 G16 K20 R4 B20 R4 B4 R4 B8 R4 B4 R4 B20 R4 K20 W6 K6 W32 K4 **R/6**

MacDonald—weathered colors

76

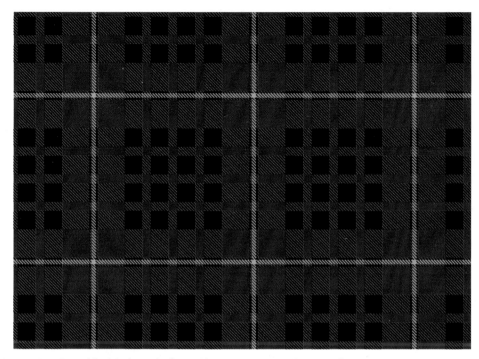

MacDonald of Ardnamurchan: R/16 K32 R16 K32 R48 K4 **Y/4**

MacDonald of Boisdale: W/4 B24 W4 R16 LG4 G24 LG4 R16 LG4 G64 LG4 R96 W4 B128 W4 R24 W4 B24 W4 **R/32**

MacDonald of Borodale: R/12 B6 R6 B64 K60 G60 Y6 **R/6**

MacDonald of Clanranald: B/32 R6 B8 R12 B48 R6 G48 W4 G20 R12 G8 R6 **G/32**

MacDonald of Clanranald, *Vestiarium Scoticum* version: **B/16** R8 B24 R2 K24 G24 R6 G4 R2 G8 **W/2**

MacDonald of Clanranald, "Old": K/16 G8 R8 G6 R64 G6 R8 G6 R8 **K/8**

MacDonald of Glenaladale, 1772: B/6 W4 R56 R12 W4 R12 G56 R56 B4 W4 **...**

MacDonald of Glenaladale, John: B/10 W4 R52 G42 R10 W4 R10 B52 R52 W4 B10 W4 R52 B52 R10 W4 R10 G42 R52 B10 **W/4**

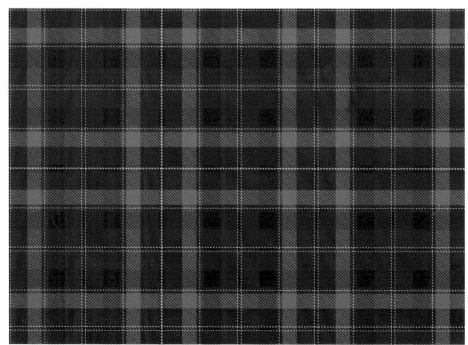

MacDonald of Glencoe: R/16 K32 R16 K32 R48 K4 **Y/4**

MacDonald of Keppoch, taken from a plaid given to Prince Charles by Keppoch: R/8 B4 R56 G48 R32 B4 R8 B4 R24 G8 **R/32**

MacDonald of Keppoch: G/4 R4 B4 R48 B12 R6 G23 R8 **B/4**

MacDonald of Keppoch: R/6 K4 R40 G32 R26 K4 R6 K4 R20 G4 **R/20**

MacDonald of Keppoch, as pictured in the McIan illustrations: R/12 K2 R2 K2 R48
K2 R2 G48 R24 G4 R4 G4 R4 G8 **R/48**

MacDonald of Kingsburgh: R/6 G6 Y4 R36 W4 G42 Y4 G4 **Y/6**

MacDonald of Sleat: DR/76 B4 DR10 DG32 DR10 B4 DR76

MacDonald of Staffa: R/32 G4 R4 G4 R4 G4 R4 G4 R12 G4 B4 G12 B4 R4 G4 R8 G4
R4 B8 R8 W4 R8 G8 W4 G8 R4 G4 R12 G4 R16 **W/4**

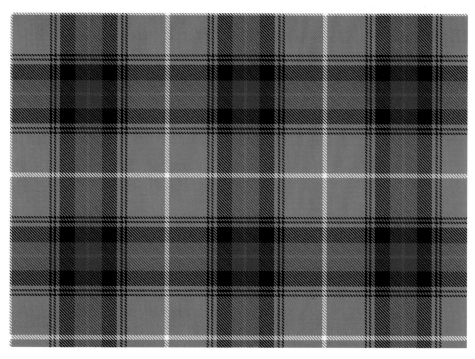

MacDonald of the Isles: W/8 G60 K4 G4 K4 G6 K24 B20 **R/6**

MacDonald, Lord of the Isles: K/4 R36 G4 R10 **G/32**

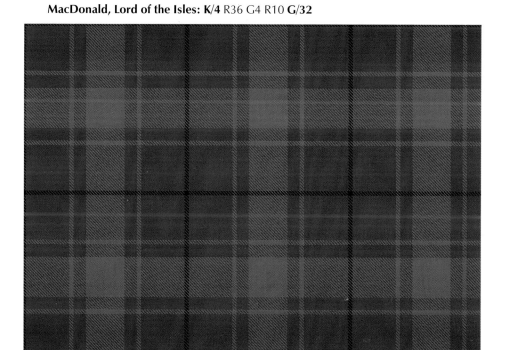

MacDonald, old sett: B/44 R12 B36 R6 K44 G56 R12 G12 R8 **G/48**

MacDonald, old sett variation: W/16 B28 R28 B84 R12 K84 G84 R28 G16 R12 **G/36**

81

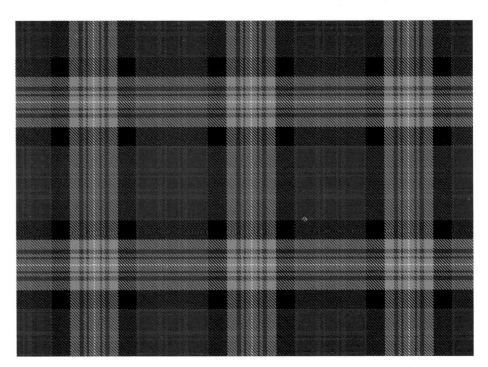

MacDonald, from a fragment found in Glencoe: G/8 Y2 R8 G4 R84 A2 B20 R10 G60 R4 B4 Y2 **R/10**

MacDonald, Dress, blue muted colors (Note: This complex tartan is non-repeating): W/16 LB8 W24 LB4 LT4 B4 W24 LB8 W8 T6 LT4 LB6 LT8 LB4 LT4 LB16 LT4 LB4 LT8 LB16 LT4 T16 A24 LT8 A4 LT4 A8 LT4 A4 LT8 A24 T16 **...**

MacDonell of Glengarry: B/32R6 B8 R12 B48 R6 K48 G24 R12 G8 R6 G14 **W/4**

MacDonell of Glengarry, Dress "Old": G/56 R8 G6 R6 B20 R6 G6 R80 G4 R6 **G/20**

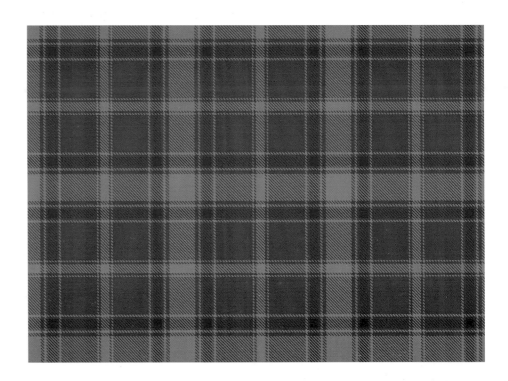

MacDougall, as woven by Lochcarron Mills: W/4 C4 R2 G28 R6 G4 R6 B12 C4 R4 C4
G12 R16 G12 R4 B4 R28 C4 R4 **W**/4
MacDougall, Smibert collection: K/4 R16 G32 R8 G4 R8 B16 R8 W4 R4 W4 R8 G16
R12 G16 R4 K4 R32 W4 **R**/144

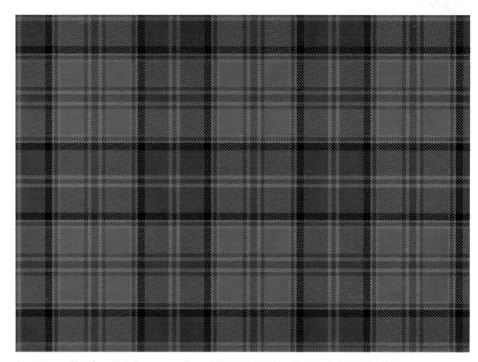

MacDougall, *Clan Originaux* **version: R**/8 C6 R40 K12 C4 R6 G40 R6 C6 **R**/12

MacDougall, Logan's version: A/4 DR8 C12 DR144 VB8 DR16 G36 DR36 G36 C24
DR8 C24 B36 DR16 G8 DR16 G144 DR8 C24 **W**/4

MacDougall: A/2 C12 R8 G50 R10 G6 R10 P24 C16 R6 C16 G24 R24 G24 R6 P6 **R/60**

MacDuff, Hunting: R/8 DT44 B40 K36 G44 DT44 R4 **DT/44**

MacDuff: K/8 R32 B32 K32 G32 R32 K4 **R/32**

MacDuff, Dress: R/8 MB4 W44 B8 W12 K24 G32 R16 K4 **R/16**

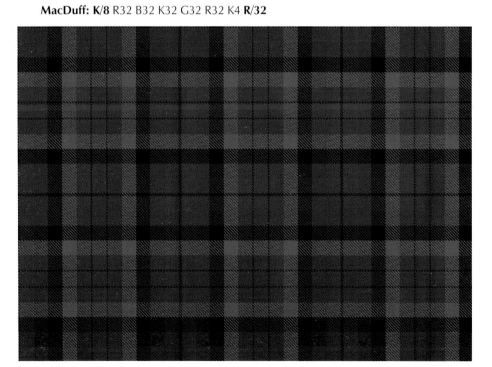

MacDuff, Dress, variation: R/10 K4 R10 K12 W4 K4 W10 K2 **Y/4**

MacEachain: LP/8 DG24 K8 B24 K4 **DR/8**

MacDuff, *Vestiarium Scoticum* **version: R/8** K8 R48 K12 B12 G32 **R/6**

MacEdward, J.C. Thompson collection: R/4 B24 G8 B6 G10 B8 G24 R38 Y4 **R/12**

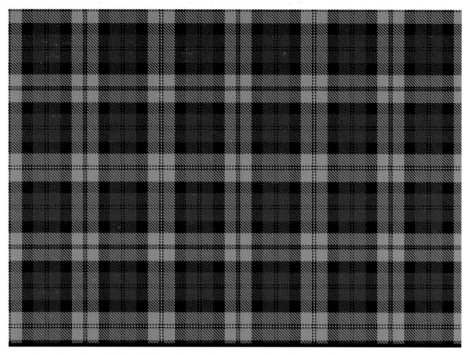

MacEwen: Y/4 K4 G24 K24 B24 K4 B4 K4 B24 K24 G24 K4 **R/4**

MacEwen arisaid: R/6 K4 W36 B36 K6 B6 K6 B36 K6 W36 K4 **Y/6**

MacFadyen: K/4 B36 K36 N36 R12 **N/20**4 K4 **LT/18**

MacFadzean: G/8 B44 W4 K44 G44 R6 **G/6**

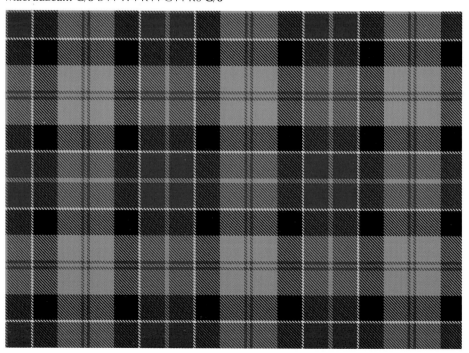

86

MacFarlane: R/84 K4 G24 W4 R6 K4 R6 W4 G4 P24 K8 R6 W8 **G/6**

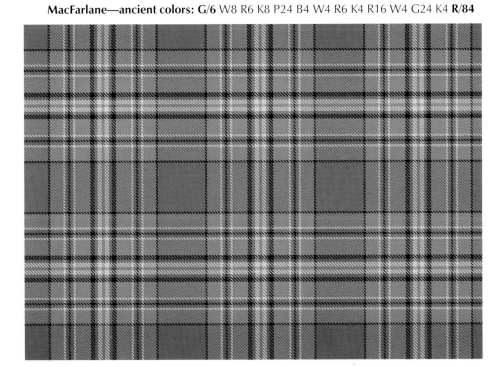

MacFarlane—ancient colors: G/6 W8 R6 K8 P24 B4 W4 R6 K4 R16 W4 G24 K4 **R/84**

MacFarlane, Black and White: K/4 W12 K4 **W/12**

MacFarlane, Hunting: G/84 K4 G24 W4 R6 K4 R6 W4 K4 B24 K8 R6 W8 **K/6**

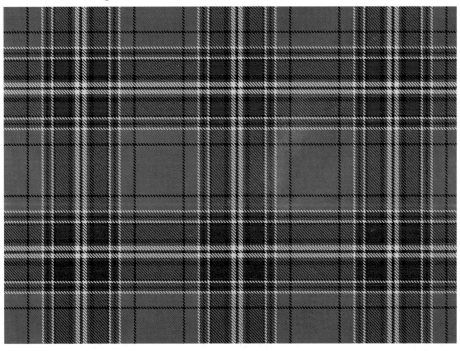

MacFarlane, Hunting—reproduction colors

MacFie, Hunting: W/4 T48 G8 R8 G64 R8 G8 T48 **Y/4**

MacFie: W/4 R48 G8 R4 G64 R4 G8 R48 **Y/4**

MacGillivray: R/8 LB4 MB4 R64 LB4 R4 MB24 R4 G32 R8 LB4 R8 **MB/4**

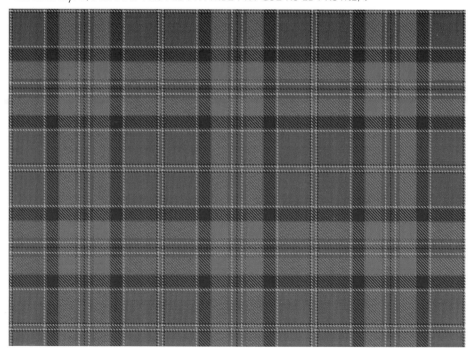

MacGlashan, "New" sett: R/80 K6 W4 LT50 W4 Y10 R8 K4 R8 Y10 W6 A8 K10 R12 W2 **A/2**

MacGlashan, "Old"—non-repeating sett: DOrange/4 DY12 DO4 DY24 DO12 DY4 DO20 DT4 LN12 DT4 LN24 DT12 LN4 DT20 **…**

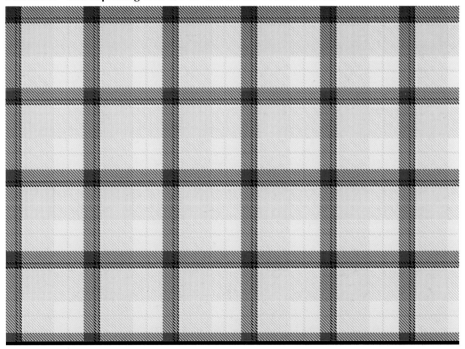

MacGlashan, alternative: R/48 K4 W4 N12 W4 Y4 R4 K4 R4 Y4 W4 LB12 K4 R6 Y6 **W/4**

MacGrath—non-repeating sett: B/8 K2 B2 K2 N24 Y10 N2 Y12 **…**

MacGregor: **R**/72 G36 R8 G12 K2 **W/4**

MacGregor—reproduction colors

MacGregor of Deeside or of Glengyle: **B/4** R8 B28 R28 B4 **R/4**

MacGregor of Glen Strae: **K/4** R32 DG36 R8 **DG/36**

MacGregor, color reversal, Alex Lumsden collection: **G/48** R16 G8 R12 K2 **W/4**

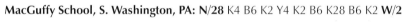

MacGuffy School, S. Washington, PA: **N/28** K4 B6 K2 Y4 K2 B6 K28 B6 K2 **W/2**

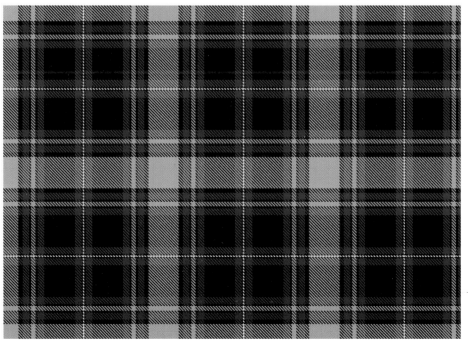

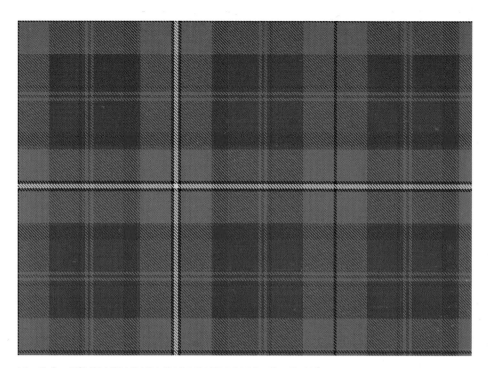

MacGuire: **K/4** G36 R36 B4 R4 G4 R4 G4 R36 B16 R4 G36 K4 **W/36**

MacHardie: **G/12** R12 B64 W8 B64 G72 R12 **B/12**

MacIan / MacKean: R/8 K16 R8 K16 R24 K4 **Y/4**

MacInnes: Y/4 K24 G4 K4 G4 K4 G32 K6 LB6 K6 B24 G12 **Y/4**

MacInnes—reproduction colors

MacInroy: K/4 G12 K12 R4 B12 R4 B4 R12 G4 **K/4**

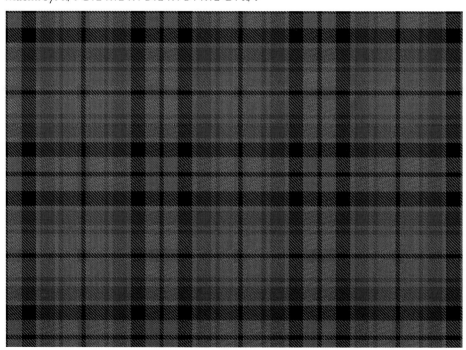

92

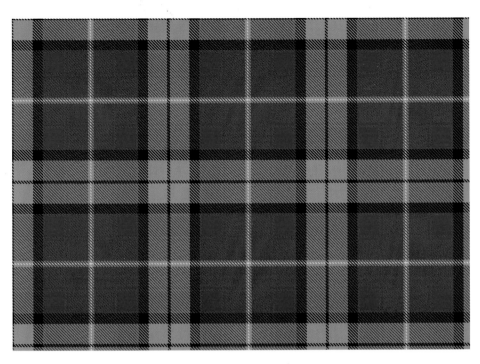

MacInroy of Lude: K/12 G68 K36 R8 B68 R8 B8 R68 G8 **W/8**

MacIntyre: A/6 R6 K6 R8 G32 R6 K6 R16 K6 R6 B32 R8 K6 R6 **A/6**

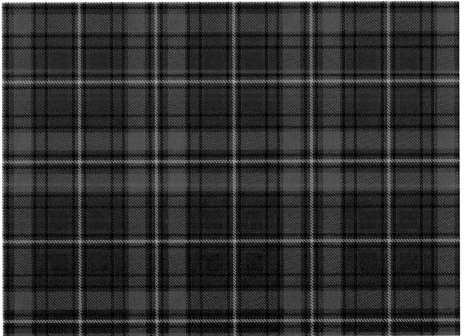

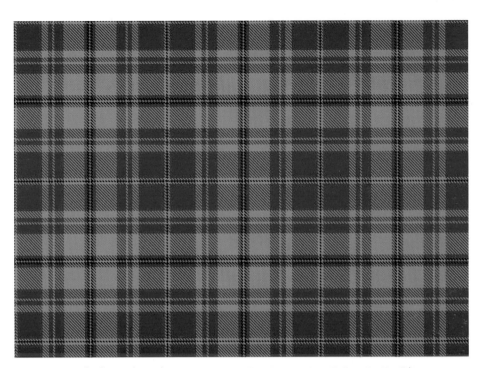

MacIntyre and Glenorchy: K/4 G4 R6 B36 R4 G12 R8 LB4 B12 R G36 R6 K4 **G/4**

MacIntyre of Whitehouse: LB/2 R4 G4 R8 B32 R4 G4 R8 B4 R4 G32 R8 B4 R4 **LB/2**

MacIntyre, *Vestiarium Scoticum* version: **W/8** G64 B24 R6 B24 **G/8**

MacIntyre, *Clan Originaux* version: **A/4** R4 K4 R4 G16 R2 K2 R4 K2 R2 B16 R4 K4 R4 **A/4**

MacIntyre, Hunting—reproductions colors

MacIver: **W/4** R24 K6 R6 K32 R6 K6 R24 **Y/4**

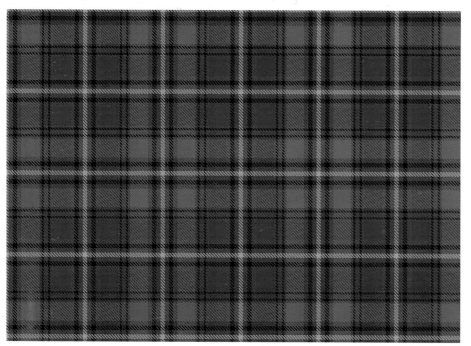

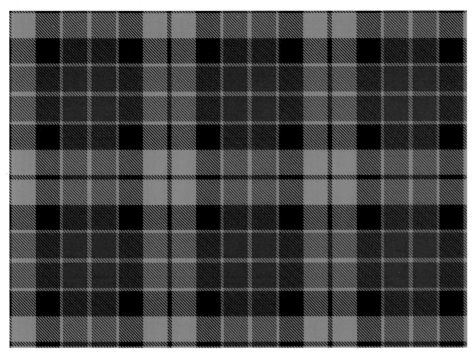

MacKay: K/6 G28 K28 G4 B28 **G/6**

MacKay, Wilson's early 1800s version

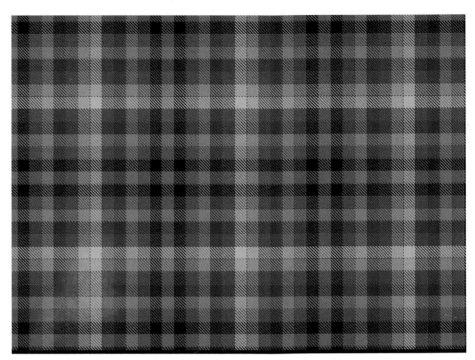

MacKay of Strathnaver: G/38 R2 K38 R2 DN38 R2 N38 R2 DT38 R2 T38 R2 LT38 R2 Cream38 R2 T38 R2 N38 R2 DN38 R2 K38 R2 **G/38**

MacKay, "Blue": R/2 B32 K12 B4 K12 **B/4**

MacKellar: W/6 B52 A4 K28 G8 W4 G6 Y8 G6 W4 **G/56**

MacKellar—weathered colors

MacKenzie: B/24 K4 B4 K4 B4 K24 G24 K4 W4 K4 G24 K24 B24 K4 **R/4**

MacKenzie, Dress: W/12 DB4 W24 DB4 W16 K12 G12 K4 W6 K4 G12 K12 B12 **R/6**

MacKenzie—weathered colors

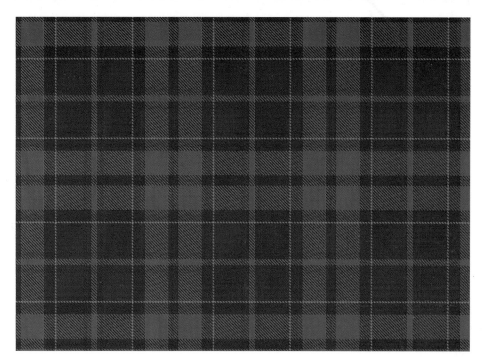

MacKillop: B/4 R4 G24 R4 B8 LB2 R28 B4 R4 **G/8**

MacKerral of Hillhouse: Y/6 DB98 LB56 **W/6**

MacKinlay: B/8 K4 B20 K20 G20 K4 **R/6**

MacKinnon: W/4 R8 P4 G16 R32 G4 B8 R4 G32 R12 B4 G4 R6 **P/4**

MacKinnon, Hunting: W/4 DT32 DG32 R4 DG32 DT32 **DG/4**

Mackintosh: R/48 B12 R6 G24 R8 **B/4**

Mackintosh, Hunting: B/4 R8 G24 R6 B12 G24 **Y/4**

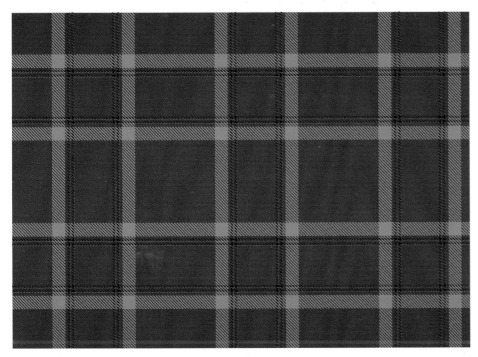

Mackintosh, as found in *Old and Rare Scottish Tartans*: R/150 G24 R6 K4 R4 K4 **R/72**

MacLachlan: R/32 K4 R4 K4 R4 K32 B32 G6 B32 K32 R32 K4 **R/4**

MacKusick: B/8 K20 G14 P6 G18 K2 B4 R2 B20 W4 P10 K2 **P/4**

MacLachlan—weathered colors

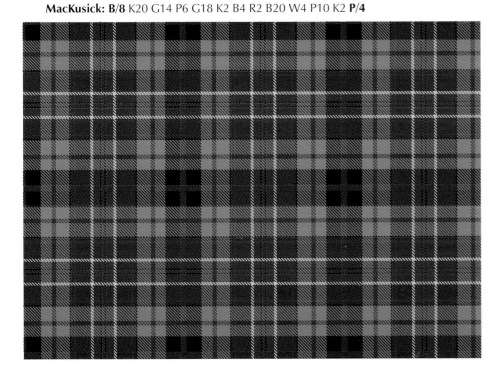

MacLachlan, "Old", c. 1800: **Y/6** W4 K32 G32 Y6 W4 **R/48**

MacLachlan, "Chief": **Y/12** K4 Y48 K12 Y4 K12 Y4 **K/12**

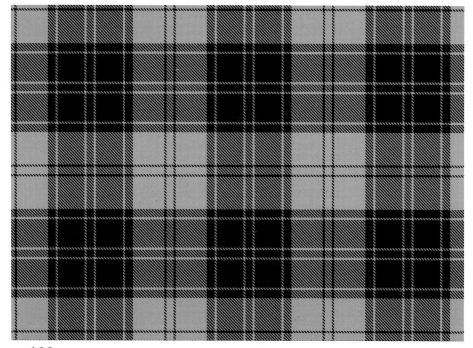

MacLachlan, Hunting

MacLachlan, "Old"—reproduction colors

MacLachlan—weathered colors

MacLaggan: **K/4** B28 K28 G24 W4 G24 **K/28**

MacLaine of Lochbuie: **R/64** G16 LB8 **Y/4**

MacLaine of Lochbuie, Hunting: **B/64** R6 B8 K4 **Y/6**

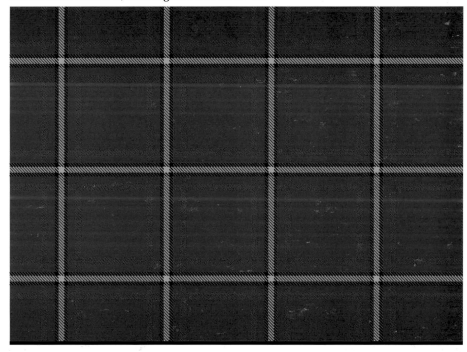

MacLaren: B/48 K16 G16 R4 G16 K4 **Y/4**

MacLaren—reproduction colors

MacLaurin of Broich: B/96 K24 G8 R8 G16 K4 **Y/8**

MacLean of Duart: K/4 R8 A4 R48 G32 K4 W4 K4 Y4 K12 A4 **B/16**

MacLean of Duart—weathered colors

MacLean of Duart—reproduction colors

MacLean of Duart, Hunting: K/4 G32 K4 G4 K12 W4 K12 **G/6**

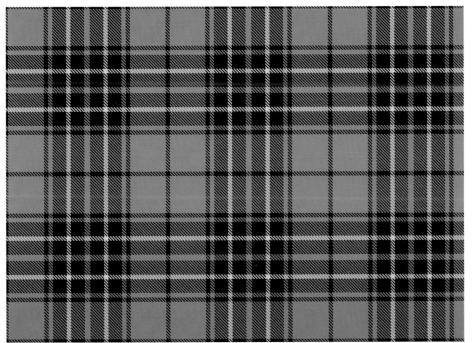

MacLeay / MacClay: R/56 G8 K8 G8 K8 B12 **Y/2**

MacLeish, McGregor-Hastie collection: K/36 B24 K10 G8 R12 G24 K4 **Y/8**

MacLennan: R/6 B6 R6 B6 R6 B16 K20 G16 R4 K4 **Y/6**

MacLellen/MacClellen: B/60 K32 G12 R12 G20 K8 Y8 K8 G20 R12 G12 K32 B16 **K/8**

MacLeod of Harris: R/6 K4 G30 K20 B40 K4 **Y/4**

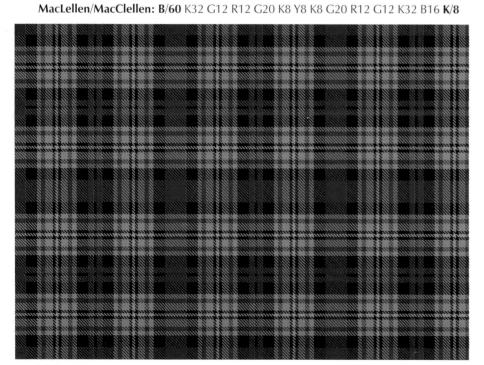

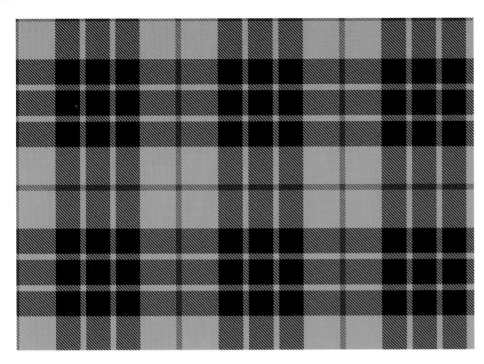

MacLeod of Lewis: R/4 Y24 K16 Y4 **K/16**

MacLeod of Gesto: K/4 W4 R8 K4 Y2 W4 Y2 K4 G20 W2 P2 R6 Y2 MT4 W4 MT4 Y4 R2 K4 W2 A6 W2 **R/68**

MacLeod of Raasay: R/4 K48 R36 K4 **R/36**

MacLeod of Skye: B/36 K4 B4 K4 B4 K28 G32 K4 Y8 K4 G32 K28 B32 K4 **R/8**

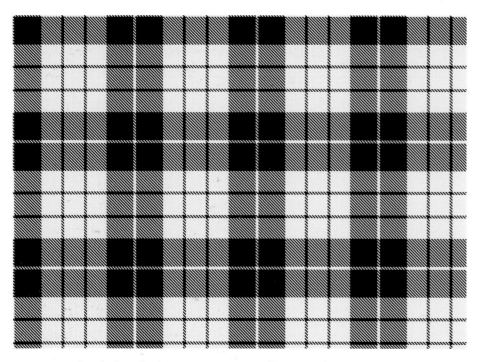

MacLeod, "Black and White," Ross Craven collection: W/4 K38 W28 K4 **W/28**

MacLeod—weathered colors

MacLeod's Highlanders (71ST Highland Light Infantry): R/4 K4 B24 K24 G24 K4 W4 K4 G24 K24 W4 R4 W4 R4 **B/24**

MacLoughlin of Ardmarnoch: G/4 K4 G12 K24 R4 K24 G4 K4 G4 K4 **G/10**

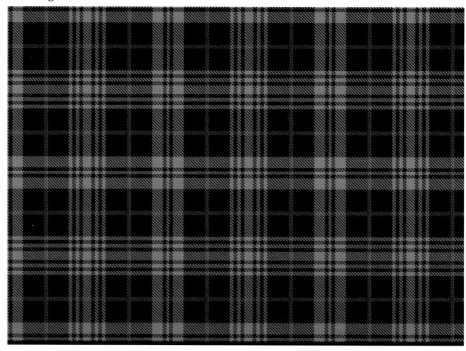

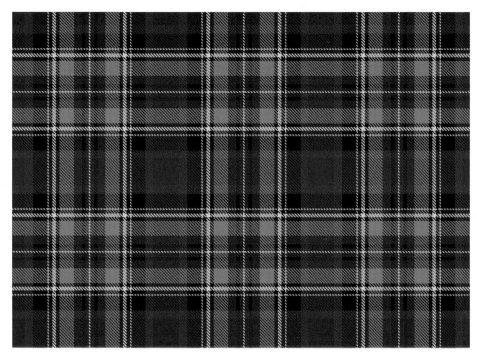

MacLullich, McGregor-Hastie collection: B/58 R16 K28 Y4 K8 W8 K8 G28 B16 K8 B8 **W/4**

MacMaster(s): A/4 K4 R56 G4 R4 G24 **W/8**

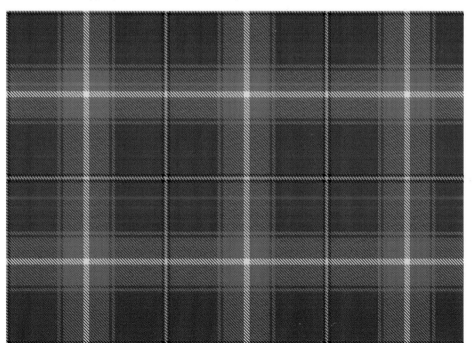

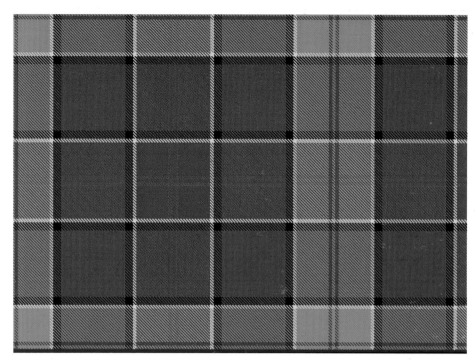

MacMichael: G/4 B4 G32 W4 K8 B32 K8 W4 R32 B4 **R/4**

MacMillan—ancient (non-reversing sett):G/8 G72 K4 G8 K4 C48 G16 Y24 K4 Y24 K4 …

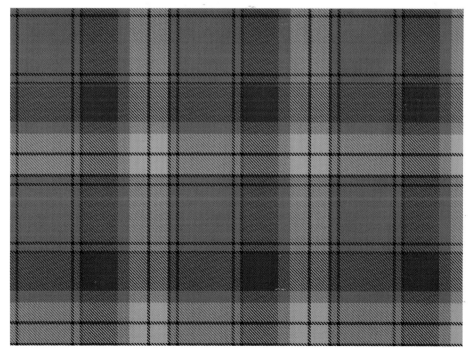

MacMillan—reproduction colors

MacMillan, "Old"—reversing sett: K/8 Y/24 K8 G12 K8 G52 R20 K4 **R/16**

MacMillan, Dress: R/4 Y16 R4 Y16 R6 Y4 R24 Y4 **R/6**

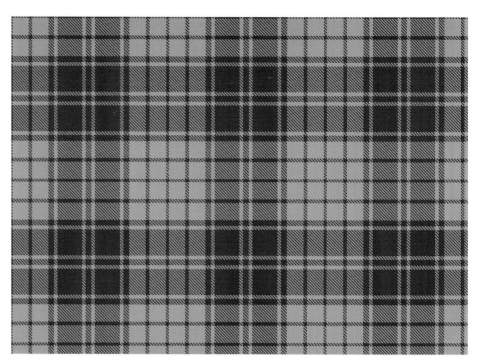

MacMillan, Hunting: R/4 G16 R4 G16 K8 Y4 K8 B24 Y4 **B/6**

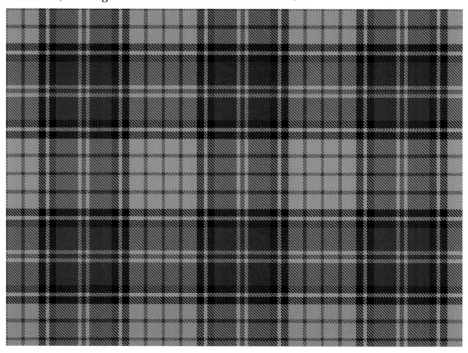

MacMillan—weathered colors

MacNab: G/16 R4 G4 R4 G4 R12 C16 R4 C16 R12 G14 C4 **G**/4

MacNab, "Old": DR/48 G4 A4 G4 **R**/48

MacNaughton: K/4 B4 R32 B16 K24 G32 R32 B4 **K**/4

MacNaughton—weathered colors

MacNeil of Gigha & Colonsay: K/4 B12 K13 G12 W4 G12 **B/8**

MacNeil of Barra: Y/6 K4 G24 K24 B28 **W/6**

MacNeil, Logan's sett: Y/4 K10 G24 K24 B24 **W4**

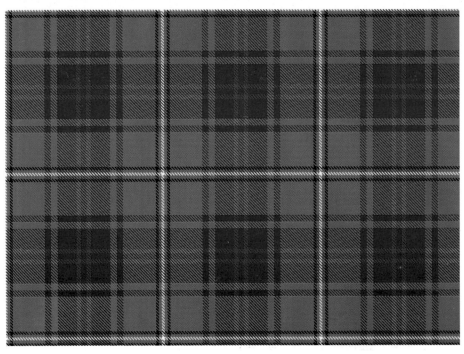

MacNeil, "Red Line": Y/4 K6 G30 K28 B32 R4 **W/4**

MacNeil, *Vestiarium Scoticum* **version: W/8** DG8 K8 DG80 B16 DG16 B48 R12 **B/6**